I fled Him, down the nights and down the days;
I fled Him, down the arches of the years;
I fled Him, down the labyrinthine ways
Of my own mind; and in the midst of tears
I hid from Him. . .
From those strong feet that followed,
followed after.
But with unhurrying chase,
And unperturbed pace,
Deliberate speed, majestic instancy,
They beat—and a voice beat
More instant than the feet—
"All things betray thee, who betrayest Me."

—From "The Hound of Heaven," Francis Thompson

TELL IT LiKE iT iS

The Gospel of John in "Living New Testament" paraphrase combined with personal views and experiences of present day people from all walks of life who have experienced Jesus Christ and seek to communicate Him effectively to others. Plus excerpts from "How to Give Away Your Faith," Paul Little, Inter-Varsity Press.

Edited by Fritz Ridenour
Illustrated by Joyce Thimsen
Research: Georgiana Walker

A Division of G/L Publications
Glendale, California, U.S.A.

Scripture quoted from *Living New Testament* is copyrighted by
Tyndale House Publishers, 1967 and is used by permission.
Excerpts and quotations from books and magazines are used
by permission from the publishers.

Over 170,000 in print
Second Printing, 1968
Third Printing, 1969
Fourth Printing, 1969

© Copyright 1968 G/L Publications

Printed in U.S.A.

Published by
Regal Books Division, G/L Publications
Glendale, California, U.S.A.

Library of Congress Catalog Card No. 68-29315
SBN 8307-0039-0

Contents

A teaching and discussion guide for use with this book is available from your Sunday School Supplier or your local Christian Bookstore.

Contents

Foreword

Tell It Like It Is is a book that seeks to do just that. It is based on the Gospel of John, because, in a special way, John was seeking to "tell it like it is" about Jesus Christ—who He really is and what He has done for all of us.

To help communicate John's message as clearly as possible, we used Ken Taylor's *Living New Testament* paraphrase of John—a masterpiece of simplicity that speaks for itself as it "tells it like it is" for today's readers.

To apply John's Gospel account to present day life, the stories, statements, and personal experiences of dozens of people are woven in with John's Gospel—twentieth century commentary that confirms John's purpose in writing his account: " . . . but these are recorded so that you will believe that He is the Messiah, the Son of God, and that believing in Him you will have Life" (John 20:31, *Living New Testament*).

In *Tell It Like It Is* you will meet the small and the great, the famous, the unknown. For example: teen-age murderer, Raul Vasquez; Angelo, a surfer who had no home but a cave on a California beach; United States Senator Mark Hatfield; all-pro linebacker Don Shinnick; Felipe Alou, major league baseball star; Tom Skinner, one-time leader of the Harlem Lords, one of the roughest teen-age gangs in New York; Dr. Howard M. Kelly, internationally known surgeon.

There are viewpoints from the clergy, too, including hard hitting ideas from Richard Halverson, Jess Moody, and Peter Marshall.

There is the Viet Nam chaplain who risked his life in the rice paddies for his men, even though he didn't have to. There are collegians who found life empty and meaningless until they turned to Christ. There are G.I.'s, a fighter pilot, an Aussie private who went to death under a Samurai sword confidently and serenely because he knew Christ.

There is Pam McGinley, teen-ager who lived a ringing testimony for Christ before she succumbed to leukemia. There is the story of the forty brave soldiers for Christ who died as martyrs under a Roman persecution.

To close *Tell It Like It Is*, we use a poem by Dr. Samuel Shoemaker which sums up the purpose of the entire book as perhaps no other piece of writing could.

In an appendix are still more ideas on sharing Christ from the personal experiences of Paul Little, author of *How to Give Away Your Faith*.

There are the ideas and stories of many others. They are all people. They are all persons who have encountered the Person of Jesus Christ. If you have not met Him, perhaps this book will help. If you have, perhaps this book will help you find new courage and know-how to "tell it like it is."

Fritz Ridenour
Youth Editor, Gospel Light Publications

"Christianity is negative—it's just a bunch of don'ts and rules to keep you from having a good time."

"Christians are really out of it. They're always judging you and looking down on you because they think they're so religious."

"Christians don't make much sense to me. They use a lot of clichés and jargon, and I can't make head or tail out of it."

Remarks like those above are often made by people who misunderstand the Christian faith and misunderstand the efforts of Christians to tell them about Christ. A definite "communication gap" exists between the typical Christian and the world that he is supposed to witness to, according to the commandments of Scripture.

As never before Christians must come to grips with the basic problem. How can they learn to "tell it like it is"? The "it" in this case is the Gospel, the old, old story that you would think Christians would know well enough by now so they could communicate it effectively. But, maybe that is just the trouble. The story *is* an "old, old story," and Christians are still using old, old ways of telling it.

Many Christians are "hung-up" on the horns of a real dilemma when it comes to "witnessing." Many of them have heard all their lives that a good Christian should witness and that a good Christian must witness and that a bad Christian does not witness. And so, they go out and try to witness to someone in their own strength—out of a sense of guilt or regimented duty.

Or, what is probably far more common, they do nothing at all. They keep their mouths shut and hope that "their lives will be a witness to others."

But the fact is that "witnessing" is not all talk or is it all action. It is a combination of both. Witnessing is not a spiritual chore or a mechanical religious exercise. A Christian witness, or to be more correct, testimony, is the sharing of the person of Christ with another person. A Christian is not only seeking to "tell it like it is," but he is seeking to tell it like it is between himself and Jesus Christ.

A Christian must have a genuine and healthy relationship with Jesus Christ or he will have no witness. He must know Jesus personally and intimately. He must know who Jesus is, what He did, why He did it. Too much Christian witnessing is simply going through the motions—telling people that they are "dirty sinners" and "here's how you can get saved, brother." This approach may have worked in the past with some people (and it has failed in the past with some people). This approach

2

CAN A CHRISTIAN GET AWAY
FROM SOUNDING ALMOST TOTALLY NEGATIVE?

may still work today with some people (but it seems to be failing with a great deal more people).

How can a Christian learn to witness effectively today? How can a Christian learn to "tell it like it is" about Christianity and Jesus Christ? How does a person get beyond the don'ts (no thanks, I don't smoke, I don't drink, I don't tell dirty jokes, I don't ... etc., etc., etc.) to the positive aspects of being a Christian? In other words, how does a Christian come through to another person and sound like his faith is something that is really vital and useful and wonderful?

The answer is simple—perhaps too simple. If you want to learn how to talk about Christ, find a book that tells you about Him. Find a book written by a man who knew Christ so well that he can introduce you to Him so that you may know Him personally too.

There is such a book, a book that does "tell it like it is." It was written by a man who faced many of the problems that Christians face today. This man lived in a pagan, secular and materialistic society.

3

He lived among people who didn't understand his particular religious jargon. He lived among people who were sophisticated, hard, jaded and cynical, and completely caught up in the values of the world. And yet, these people were searching—just as people are searching today—searching for an answer to life and a way to fill the emptiness inside with something besides a continual grasping for things and sensual pleasure.

The man? The apostle John.

The book? The Gospel according to John.

John wrote his Gospel after the other three Gospels (Matthew, Mark and Luke) were done. John was an old man at the time. For over 50 years he had meditated upon what Christ had taught him and upon his personal experience with Jesus Christ as he had lived, eaten and talked with Him daily for some three years.

John lived in Ephesus—a Greek speaking and thinking community far from Jerusalem and the typical Jewish tradition and culture. John realized that there were thousands of Greek converts to Christianity who would not understand the more Jewishly oriented Gospels written by Matthew, Mark and Luke. John knew that these new Christians, who had been converted from a background of paganism, needed a Gospel that would tell them exactly who Christ was and what He had actually done for men everywhere.

John made no bones about the fact that he wrote his Gospel in order to help people believe in Christ and have life through His name (John 20:31). John's Gospel is completely different from the other three

4

accounts, which give a much more general or over-all view of Christ's life. John is unique in his presentation because he presents Christ as God and explains what it means to be a Christian as perhaps no other Biblical writer.

It is for this reason that the Gospel of John has been used as the major portion of *Tell It Like It Is*. In order to "tell it like it is" as clearly as possible for today's reader, the text of John has been repro-duced in Ken Taylor's famed *Living New Testa-ment* paraphrase.

Woven into the text of John's Gospel as illustra-tive commentary are numerous true incidents, per-sonal testimonies, and other anecdotal material to help focus John's tremendous book on the basic challenge to witness faced by every Christian in today's space-age society. Also, each chapter offers ideas to help the Christian take stock of his own spiritual condition and motivation as well as ideas on how to improve his own witnessing methods and techniques.

THE CHRISTIAN SHOULD WITNESS TO PEOPLE, NOT TARGETS

In an appendix to the book, additional ideas on witnessing are presented by Paul Little, Director of Evangelism for Inter-Varsity Christian Fellowship. Mr. Little has had many years of experience in sharing the Gospel—particularly with those on the college campus. He has personally experienced the frustration and fear that comes from trying to witness out of a guilt complex and in a clumsy and offensive way. He has learned by hard experience some techniques and basic rules of communication that can help any Christian more effectively communicate his faith.

Above all, Paul Little has learned that people are persons, not targets or trophies or simply "souls to be won for Jesus." It is true enough that every person is a soul and that he needs to hear about Christ. The danger in using this term, however, is to slip into the impersonal attitude that people are souls to be added to the Christian workers list, much as scalps were once added to Geronimo's belt. If this happens there is the possibility of not seeing a person as a real person, not treating him as a human being should be treated. Jesus Himself always talked to the whole man and was well aware of every person's humanity and human predicament. Jesus saw people as not simply "souls to be won" but as people who needed to be saved and He went about saving whole people with souls, not statistics that were given the title of soul.

And so, let us begin. Let us begin at the beginning of John's Gospel. John knew that there is no better way to tell it like it is than to begin at the beginning . . .

CHAPTER 2

There can't be a God . . . or can there?

The scene is a typical English literature class—typical in the sense that guys like Jim are bored to tears because they are bored stiff with school in general. But suddenly Jim comes up with one of his "class shakers." He barges in on a polite discussion of some innocent little line such as Robert Frost's, "And they, since they were not the one dead, turned to their affairs."

"Did Frost believe in God?" asks Jim.

Suddenly the tame discussion of English literature has turned into a fascinating conversation about religion.

"There can't be a God," says Bill wistfully, "I wish there could, but there can't."

Barbara's hand flashes up. "How can you be so dogmatic? You'd have to know everything that there is before you could say what isn't."

A guy named Shaffer is next to speak. His mind is usually "off somewhere" in these sessions, but like Jim, a discussion like this turns him on. He says,

7

"Where is He then, if there is a God? Science can't find Him."

Bob's hand goes up next. "That ain't a very hard problem."

"*Isn't*," corrects the teacher.

"Isn't," Bob repeats. "God is a spirit. Science studies matter. A scientist won't find God in matter any more than an African will find the Statue of Liberty in his grass hut."

And so it goes, a basic discussion in a secular high school classroom. The students in this true incident* are searching for answers about God. They are the same kind of answers that people were looking for when John wrote his Gospel. Just who is God? If He exists, where is He? John gets right down to cases on this basic point . . .

John 1:1-18

[1,2]Before anything else existed,[a]** there was Christ,[b] with God. He has always[c] been alive and is Himself God. [3]He created everything there is—nothing exists that He didn't make. [4]Eternal life is in Him, and this life gives light to all mankind. [5]His life is the light that shines through the darkness—and the darkness can never extinguish it.

[6,7]God sent John the Baptist as a witness to the fact that Jesus Christ is the true Light. [8]John himself was not the Light; he was only a witness to identify it.

[9]Later on, the one who is the true Light arrived to shine on everyone coming into the world. [10]But although He made the world, the world didn't recognize Him when He came. [11,12]Even in His own land and

---

*Adapted from the article, "The Adolescents' Search for God," Robert Bahr, *Eternity*, September 1967, p. 19.
**The superior letters throughout John refer to footnotes from the *Living New Testament*, Paraphrased. For footnotes see p. 233.

among His own people, the Jews, He was not accepted. Only a few would welcome and receive Him. But to all who received Him, He gave the right to become children of God. All they needed to do was to trust Him to save them.[d] [13]All those who believed this were reborn!—not a physical rebirth,[e] resulting from human passion or plan—but from the will of God.

[14]And Christ[f] became a human being and lived here on earth among us and was full of loving forgiveness[g] and truth. And some of us have seen His glory[h]—the glory of the only Son of the heavenly Father![i] [15]John pointed Him out to the people, telling the crowds, "This is the one I was talking about when I said, 'Someone is coming who is greater by far than I am— for He existed long before I did!'" [16]We have all

9

benefited from the rich blessings He brought to us—blessing upon blessing heaped upon us! ¹⁷For Moses gave us only the Law with its rigid demands and merciless justice, while Jesus Christ brought us loving forgiveness as well. ¹⁸No one has ever actually seen God, but of course His only Son has, for He is the companion of the Father and has told us all about Him.

Can you put God in focus?

A basic problem with communicating Christ to people today is terminology. The way you talk about God can either put Him in focus for someone or it can leave him fuzzy, confused, or just downright fed up with Christians and their clichés.

The hippies—flower child phenomena of the 1960's—are a good example of people who are fed up. They claim they are fed up with just about everything: the hypocrisy of the establishment, the pressure of the materialistic rat race, and even the brand of Christianity preached by some churches. But their disenchantment with the church didn't clear up their fuzzy ideas about God. There is, for example, the story of "Groovy," alias James L. Hutchinson, a hard core hippie who was murdered in a Greenwich village basement along with Linda Fitzpatrick, another hippie disciple, in the summer of 1967.

Groovy is reported to have told a magazine reporter that he didn't believe in churches, "Just in Christ. I see him as a man just like me, trying to live without hate."

Scrawled over the doorway of the hippie hangout where Groovy spent most of his time was a sign reading "J. C. Guards This Place." J. C. stood for

"DO-IT-YOURSELF CHRISTIANITY" DOESN'T PUT GOD IN FOCUS

Jesus Christ, and as a "disciple" and receiver of Christ's protection, Groovy returned the Lord's favor with a police record that included drunkenness as well as assault with a dangerous weapon, impairing morals of a minor and possession of narcotics.

The point of this story is not to criticize hippies, but to show that there can be a vast gulf between the Bible's clear-cut description of God and Jesus Christ and subjective "do-it-yourself Christianity." It is easy for anyone to criticize the "hypocrisy of the establishment," especially the hypocrisy of the established church. It is just as easy for anyone—hippie or otherwise—to slip into his own particular brand of hypocrisy because he chooses to draw his own fuzzy picture of God and Jesus Christ.*

Consider the difference between Groovy's opinion of Jesus and the opinion of Dr. Richard Halver-

*See "Trying to Live without Hate," Point and Counterpoint, Bruce Shelley, *Action*, January, 1968.

son, writer of a nationally circulated weekly devotional letter for businessmen:

Jesus Christ is the *final — absolute — incontrovertible* ground for Christian faith ...

If He can be discredited—Christianity is discredited ...

If He is wrong—Christianity is wrong ...

If He can fail—Christianity will fail!

Christian faith *rises and falls with Jesus Christ!*

Not our doctrine about Him—but Jesus Christ Himself.

Our doctrine is fallible—He is not.

Our doctrine may be wrong—He is not.

Put all the theology together—every thought man has ever formulated about Jesus Christ—He is *greater by infinity than the sum total* of all dogma conceived by the mind of man.

You cannot escape Jesus Christ as a fact of history ...

He was actually born in a certain place at a certain time under certain conditions ...

He lived a certain kind of life—taught many things—did many things ...

And finally *died as a common criminal* in the method most accepted in that day for capital punishment.

History is divided by Him. In the words of Charles Malik of Lebanon, "Jesus Christ is the hinge of history."

The fact of Jesus Christ's existence is indisputable ...

But the minute you accept Him as a fact of history—*you cannot explain Him on any other grounds* than that He was God in the flesh!

He was unique in His birth ...

He was unique in His life ...

He was unique in His death ...

He was unique in His victory over death—the resurrection.*

The apostle John put the whole thing sharply in

Perspective, Volume 19, No. 13, April 12, 1967, Richard C. Halverson. Dr. Halverson left a promising career in entertainment to become a fulltime minister, writer, and Christian leader. He is known around the world in high government places. Besides his long-time ministry at Fourth Presbyterian Church of Washington, D. C., Dr. Halverson has published *Perspective*, his weekly newsletter for businessmen, for many years. He has served as interim president for World Vision, Inc. He has also played a key role in the development of International Christian Leadership, an organization for businessmen. He has been an active leader in the Presidential prayer breakfast in Washington, D. C.

focus as he opened his Gospel: "The word (God in Jesus Christ) became flesh and dwelt among us . . ." (John 1:14).

John 1:19-51

[19]The Jewish leaders[j] sent priests and assistant priests from Jerusalem to ask John whether he claimed to be the Messiah. [20]He denied it flatly. "I am not the Christ," he said.

[21]"Well then, who are you?" they asked. "Are you Elijah?"

"No," he replied.

"Are you the Prophet?"[k]

"No."

[22]"Then who are you? Tell us, so we can give an answer to those who sent us. What do you have to say for yourself?"

[23]He replied, "I am a voice from the barren wilderness, shouting as Isaiah prophesied, 'Get ready for the coming of the Lord!' "

[24,25]Then those who were sent by the Pharisees asked him, "If you aren't the Messiah or Elijah or the Prophet, what right do you have to baptize?"

[26]John told them, "I merely baptize with[l] water, but right here in the crowd is Someone you have never met, [27]Who will soon begin His ministry among you, and I am not even fit to be His slave." [28]This incident took place at Bethany, a village on the other side of the Jordan River where John was baptizing.

[29]The next day John saw Jesus coming toward him and said, "Look! This is the Lamb of God who takes away the world's sin! [30]This is the one I was talking about when I said 'Soon a man far greater than I am is coming who existed long before me!' [31]I didn't know He was the one, but I am here baptizing with water in order to point Him out to the nation of Israel."

[32]Then John told about seeing the Holy Spirit in

13

the form of a dove descending from heaven and resting upon Jesus. [33]"I didn't know He was the one," John said again, "but at the time God sent me to baptize, He told me, 'When you see the Holy Spirit descending and resting upon someone—He is the one you are looking for. He is the one who baptizes with the Holy Spirit.' [34]I saw it happen to this man, and I therefore testify that He is the Son of God."

[35]The following day as John was standing with two of his disciples, [36]Jesus walked by. John looked at Him intently and then declared, "See! There is the Lamb of God!" [37]Then John's two disciples turned and followed Jesus! [38]Jesus looked around and saw them following. "What do you want?" He asked them.

"Sir," they replied, "where do You live?"

[39]"Come and see," He said. So they went with Him to the place where He was staying and were with Him from about four o'clock that afternoon until the evening. [40](One of these men was Andrew, Simon Peter's brother.) [41]Andrew then went to find his brother Peter and told him, "We have found the Messiah!" [42]And he brought Peter to Jesus.

Jesus looked intently at Peter for a moment and then said, "You are Simon, John's son—but you shall be called Peter, the Rock!"

[43]The next day Jesus decided to go to Galilee. He found Philip and told him, "Come with Me." [44](Philip was from Bethsaida, Andrew and Peter's home town.) [45]Philip now went off to look for Nathanael and told him, "We have found the Messiah!—the very person Moses and the prophets told about! His name is Jesus, the son of Joseph from Nazareth!"

[46]"Nazareth!" exclaimed Nathanael, "Can anything good come from there?"

"Just come and see for yourself," Philip declared.

[47]As they approached, Jesus said, "Here comes an honest man—a true son of Israel!"

[48]"How do you know what I am like?" Nathanael demanded.

And Jesus replied, "I could see you under the fig tree before Philip found you!"

⁴⁹Nathanael replied, "Sir, You are the Son of God—the King of Israel!"

⁵⁰Jesus asked him, "Do you believe all this just because I told you I had seen you under the fig tree? You will see greater proofs than this! ⁵¹You will even see heaven open and the angels of God coming back and forth to Me, the Man of Glory.'"ᵐ

From a "nobody" named Kimball to . . .

There is a basic truth found in these verses that describes how Christ picked His disciples, those whom He would teach and live with during His earthly ministry: there is potential in every man. Christ picked 12 men who would hardly qualify for Rhodes scholarships or the "most likely to succeed" awards. Yet, God used them. He is still using ordinary men. Consider, for example, the following chain of events: An unheard of nobody named Edward Kimball once taught a Sunday School class. One of his students was a young fellow who worked at a shoe store. One day Kimball paid him a visit at the store and led him to Christ in the back room as he was putting shoes away on the shelf. That man was Dwight L. Moody, who went on to become one of the greatest preachers and evangelists of all time.

While visiting the British Isles, Moody preached in a little chapel whose pastor was a young man with the imposing name of Fredric Brotherton Meyer. During his sermon, Moody told an emotion-charged story about a Sunday School teacher he had known in Chicago who found out that he had very little time left to live and who personally went to each pupil in his class and led every one of them to a saving faith in Christ.

Pastor Meyer was unmoved by the tale, but one of the teachers of the senior girls' class in his church was so impressed that she told it to her class of girls and later reported to Meyer that "I believe every one of my girls has given her heart to God!"

The teacher's report shook Meyer to the toes and changed his entire ministry. Meyer later testified that he owed everything to that moment where for the first time he found what it meant to be broken-hearted about sin and how to point men to God.

Meyer came to America and preached many times. In a chapel talk at Furman University, he made the statement, "You never test the resources of God till you attempt the impossible." A discouraged young man who was about to drop out of school heard that remark, took new courage, and went on to get his degree. He later became one of the great orators of his time, Robert Greene Lee.

On another occasion, Meyer was preaching in Moody's school in Northfield, Mass. A confused young preacher sitting in the back row heard Meyer say, "If you are not willing to give up everything for Christ, are you willing to be made willing?" The remark changed the entire ministry of the young preacher whose name was J. Wilber Chapman.

Chapman went on to become one of the most effective evangelists of his time. When he decided to return to the pastorate he turned his ministry over to a YMCA clerk whom he had been using as an advance man to set up his crusades. This "advance man" who had learned to preach the Gospel by hearing and watching Chapman, captured the imagination of the entire country. Hundreds of thousands of people came to know Christ as they heard the preaching of Billy Sunday in the great tabernacles and large cities of the nation.

In 1924 Billy Sunday conducted a revival in Charlotte, N. C., and out of those meetings came a group of laymen determined to form a permanent organization to continue witnessing for Christ in their community. In 1932 that same group arranged for a crusade for revival at Charlotte, and brought in evangelist Mordacai Ham for city-wide meetings.

One evening a lanky 16-year-old boy sat in the huge crowd in the tabernacle and was spellbound by the message of the white-haired evangelist, who seemed to be talking and waving his long finger straight at him. The 16-year-old joined the choir where he thought he could escape, but it was no use. Finally the tall youth could stand it no longer and went forward to receive Christ. Two of his friends were saved also.

As time passed, these three young men felt called by God into the ministry. The tall one went to an obscure Bible college in Florida and later transferred to Wheaton College where he started his career in the Youth for Christ movement and went on to a world-wide evangelistic ministry. His name? Billy Graham, the man who has undoubtedly communicated Jesus Christ to more people than any other man in history.

Remember how this sequence of events started?

TALENT ISN'T THE FIRST THING
CHRIST LOOKS FOR . . .

A "nobody" named Kimball went into a shoe store to talk to one of his students about Christ. There was potential in that student, and that potential grew and multiplied. It is still growing and multiplying today.*

Jesus saw potential in the ordinary fishermen and laborers that He chose to be His disciples. He knew these men had possibilities. None of them had a great deal of "talent," but talent wasn't really what Christ was looking for then, or is He looking for it today. He uses talent, to be sure, but the qualities that Christ looks for in a person are obedience, faith, and willingness to learn.

*Adapted from the article "Passing the Torch of Evangelism," James H. Semple, *Christianity Today*, October 27, 1967, p. 15.

TAKE TIME . . .

Use the following ideas to take time to take a second look at John 1 and apply it to your life and the daily situations that only you face.

God invades humanity. Read John 1:1-14. List three reasons why you think this passage is important to an effective Christian witness. In other words, why is it worth the Christian's time to know what is in this passage and to be able to refer to it?

John the Baptist: oddity or necessity? Read John 1:15-27. John the Baptist has been called the "forerunner of Jesus." Why did Jesus Christ need a "forerunner"? What was John the Baptist's major goal when he preached? What did he ask men to do? Why is this act important?

A lamb with more power than a thousand lions. Read John 1:29-34. Would it be accurate to say that John the Baptist was the first Christian "convert"—coming even ahead of Andrew, Peter, James and John? What characteristics of the sincere believer in Christ does John the Baptist show in this passage?

Come and see. Read John 1:35-51. What basic principles in communicating Christ to others are found here? What basic characteristics of belief in Christ are shown by these men? In other words, how do these men act toward Christ? Do you see yourself in any of these men? In what way?

The same—forever. Compare John 1:1,2 with Heb. 13:8. How do these verses make you feel? Is it of any practical use to you to know that Jesus Christ is always the same and that He never changes? Why?

He made it all. Compare John 1:3 with Col. 1:16-19 and Heb. 1:3. Write down how you feel about the idea that Christ created us and then came and died for us as well. Are you grateful? Awestruck? Indifferent? Think through why you feel as you do.

Do you really have something to say? Reread John 1:1-14. How many practical benefits of being a Christian can you find in this passage? In other words, what do you find here that gives you something specific to say about the value and worth of being a Christian?

TAKE INVENTORY . . .

Take a piece of paper and write from memory the basic facts about Jesus Christ that you have thought about while reading this chapter. If Christ were not fully God, would these facts be real facts? Why?

In John 1 we learn that Christ created the world and then He came into the world but was not received by many of those He had created. But those who do receive Christ become the sons of God and are included in God's family. Have you received Christ? As Saviour? As Lord? Ask yourself: "What is different about my life because Christ is my Saviour?" And then ask yourself: "What is different about my life because Christ is my Lord?"

TAKE ACTION . . .

Write a letter to a hypothetical person (or perhaps a real friend) and explain to him just who Jesus Christ is as far as you understand the teachings of the Gospel. Ask a non-Christian to read your letter and to tell you if he understands what you are trying to say.

If you prefer talking to writing, try explaining your views on Jesus Christ to a Christian friend and then try them on a non-Christian. Explain to the non-Christian that you are trying to learn how to communicate your faith and you would appreciate any "feedback" he could give you on how you explain your views on Christ.

Both of these exercises not only test the effectiveness of your communication, but they give you opportunities to gradually do some witnessing as well.

CHAPTER 3

Why follow this man Jesus?

Yes, why follow Jesus? A good question ... especially in the past few years when there have been so many good causes ... Vista and the Peace Corps, for example, or perhaps your "bag" would be civil rights or the war on poverty.

Of course, you can always follow that other great cause—the pursuit of the almighty dollar—by leaping into today's rushing torrent of materialism, which makes the Mississippi look like a leak in a Toyota's radiator.

John knew why he followed Jesus. He knew that Jesus had power and authority to work in his life. In chapter 2 of his Gospel, John tells two simple stories that dramatically portray this power and authority ...

John 2:1-25

¹Two days later Jesus' mother was a guest at a wedding in the village of Cana in Galilee, ²And Jesus and His disciples were invited too. ³The wine supply ran out during the festivities, and Jesus' mother came to Him with the problem.

⁴"I can't help you now," He said.ⁿ "It isn't yet My time for miracles."

⁵But His mother told the servants, "Do whatever He tells you!"

⁶Six stone waterpots were standing there; they were used for Jewish ceremonial purposes and held perhaps 20 to 30 gallons each. ⁷,⁸Then Jesus told the servants to fill them to the brim with water. When this was done He said, "Dip some out and take it to the master of ceremonies." ⁹When the master of ceremonies tasted the water that was now wine, not knowing where it had come from (though, of course, the servants did), he called the bridegroom over. ¹⁰"This is wonderful stuff!" he said. "You're different from most! Usually a host uses the best wine first, and afterwards, when everyone is full and doesn't care, then he brings out the less expensive brands. But you have kept the best for the last!" ¹¹This miracle at Cana in Galilee was Jesus' first public demonstration of His heaven-sent power. And His disciples believed that He really was the Messiah.°

¹²After the wedding He left for Capernaum for a few days with His mother, brothers, and disciples. ¹³Then it was time for the annual Jewish Passover celebration, and Jesus went to Jerusalem. ¹⁴In the Temple area He saw merchants selling cattle, sheep, and doves for sacrifices, and money changers behind their counters. ¹⁵Jesus made a whip from some ropes and chased them all out, and drove out the sheep and oxen, scattering the money changers' coins over the floor and turning over their tables! ¹⁶Then, going over to the men selling doves, He told them, "Get these things out of here! Don't turn My Father's

Is the wine miracle an argument for social drinking?

A favorite conclusion drawn by some people is that because Jesus made wine at the wedding at Cana, "social drinking is all right as far as the Bible is concerned." Before anyone decides to use this as a proof text for social drinking, he should keep in mind that Jesus was in the center of His Father's will at all times. His entire earthly ministry was devoted to redeeming men from sin, reclaiming lives that had been destroyed by disease, despair, etc. To lift the wine-making incident out of context and its cultural setting (Palestine lacked decent drinking water and wine was a preservable substitute) and use it to justify the "pursuit of pleasure" by a vast host of social drinkers today is about as logical as saying that Jesus approved of violence and killing because at one point in His ministry, He told the disciples: "He who has no sword should sell his garment and go buy one" (Luke 22:36). The real point of the wine-making incident is Jesus' power. Jesus made the water into wine to help the newlyweds out of an embarrassing situation, but He also did it to strengthen the faith of His disciples, to show a sign that would give His followers further evidence that He was God Himself.

House into a market!" [17]Then His disciples remembered this prophecy from the Scriptures:

"Concern for God's House will be My undoing."

[18]"What right have you to order them out?" the Jewish leaders' demanded. "If you have this authority from God, show us a miracle to prove it."

[19]"All right," Jesus replied, "this is the miracle I will do for you: Destroy this sanctuary and in three days I will raise it up!"

[20]"What!" they exclaimed. "It took 46 years to build this Temple, and you can do it in three days?"

[21]But by "this sanctuary" He meant His body. [22]After He came back to life again, the disciples remembered His saying this and realized that what He had quoted from the Scriptures really did refer to Him and had all come true!

[23]Because of the miracles He did in Jerusalem at the Passover celebration, many people were convinced that He was indeed the Messiah. [24,25]But Jesus didn't trust them, for He knew mankind to the core. No one needed to tell Him how changeable human nature is!

23

All the right gear and no place to go

This chapter falls nicely into three parts: John 2:1-11 is the story of the making of wine at Cana. Here was Christ's first public miracle and it is a clear-cut example of His divine power. John 2:12-22 describes the "raid" on the temple racketeers, a clear-cut example of Christ's authority to speak and act as if He were God Himself because He was God Himself. John 2:23-25 is Christ's refusal to commit Himself to those whose interest in Him was superficial.

What does this chapter have to say about wit-

TOO MANY CHRISTIANS ARE LIKE THE WATER SKIER
WHO COULDN'T 'GET UP ON TOP'

nessing? About communicating Christ? Consider
the modern parable of the water skier ...

Behold, a certain young man went forth to water
ski. He prepared himself by obtaining the finest and
most expensive craft available, to which he affixed a
sturdy, strong motor. After much deliberation, he
chose a pair of the most highly-recommended skis
in the sporting goods section of a large store. The
rope was of fine-twined nylon, prepared by skilled
artisans, forasmuch as the skier wanted to be assured of its durability. He then counseled with
himself as follows: Yet suppose with all this, I
should lack proper balance in my attempts to skim
across the water? I must needs provide myself with

a life preserver, that I may not fall beneath the surface and thus drown.

Then this skier, having reasoned so, acquired a life belt from a reputable dealer, and having made himself thus equipped, transported his gear to the shores of a nearby lake. He launched the craft, complete with its motor, into the waters; and then having attired himself in the vestments of the skier, and with the rope attached to the stern of the boat he prepared to experience the joy of his endeavors. But, to his dismay, he could not "get up." Try as he would, he remained on his skis, standing to his midriff in the quiet waters.

On the shore, many of his friends marvelled among themselves, saying: "What meaneth this? How is it that he cannot 'get up'? Has he committed some grievous error in the purchase of his gear?"

But a certain man, standing nearby, approached them, wagging his head and saying: "Not so, his equipment is of the best quality and purchased at the finest stores. Yet lacketh he one thing. He hath not a helmsman in his craft to guide it about the lake." And thus saying, he made his way to the boat, and having established himself in the driver's seat, stirred the motor into action. Gracefully, the skier rose to the surface, and henceforth with great facility and to the joy of his companions, traversed the waters with ease.*

It could just be that many Christian witnesses are like this water skier. They find themselves with all

*"The Parable of the Water Skier," Collegiate Conversationals, Division of the American Tract Society, Ordell, N. J.

CASUAL INTEREST IN CHRIST WILL NEVER COMMUNICATE HIM TO OTHERS

the equipment they think they need to "get up on top and witness for Christ." That is, they believe they have desire. They believe they have a balanced view of Christ (they have their doctrine straight). But, they seem unable to move. They lack one thing—a helmsman, someone to drive the boat, someone to turn on the power necessary to put them up on top of the waves.

Casual interest in Christ will not make Him your helmsman. Superficial commitment to the Lord will never communicate who He really is. If you are not totally sold out to Christ ... if you do not recognize His power and authority in your life ... Christ will not "commit Himself to you." Without Christ at the helm, you will go nowhere.

27

TAKE TIME . . .

Use the following ideas to take time to take a second look at John 2 and apply it to your life in daily situations that you face.

The first of many miracles. Read John 2:1-11. Does this first miracle seem "significant" enough for Christ to perform? Jesus never did any miracle without a specific purpose. What do you think His purpose was here?

A matter of timing. Compare John 2:4 with John 7:6; 12:23; 17:1; Matt. 26:18; and Mark 14:41. In all of these verses the phrase "My hour" is mentioned. When Jesus talks about "My hour" to what is He referring? What does this tell you about God's timetable? How do you apply God's timetable to your own life?

Gentle Jesus meek and mild? Read John 2:12-21. What made Christ angry in this situation? Was He justified in getting so angry? Why?

Is your church a "den of thieves"? Compare John 2:13-17 with Matt. 21:12,13; Mark 11:15-18; and Luke 19:45,46. Does the "angry Christ" in these passages make you feel uncomfortable? What if Jesus came into your church and made a strong protest that bordered on physical violence? What would you think?

More authority than the "religious authorities"? Reread John 2:18-22. Did the Jewish leaders understand what Christ meant by "destroying this temple and raising it up in three days"? Did their answer to His claim show spiritual perception or preoccupation with material ideas? Why is it easier to become caught up in material thinking and not see the spiritual side? Read this passage through several times then ask yourself the following questions: "Would Jesus 'commit Himself' to me? That is, would He believe that I have real allegiance to Him and His cause? Why do I follow Jesus Christ?"

TAKE INVENTORY . . .

Evaluate your own Christian experience and see if you are a victim of any of these traps:

Is your faith "environmental" or can you honestly say

that your spiritual life doesn't depend on the same routine week after week with the same Christian friends in the same church? In other words, do you know what direct personal communication between yourself and the living God is really like? What would happen to your spiritual life if you were taken out of your present environment and placed in a completely secular, agnostic, and even anti-Christian atmosphere? Do you think your faith would grow stronger or weaker? Why?

Is your Christian faith simply a set of facts that you've arranged in neat theological order? That is, is it simply limited to some *thing* to believe? Or do you realize that Christianity is some *One* to receive? Ask yourself, "Do I know all about Jesus Christ but hardly know Him personally? How do I know that I really know Christ personally? What evidence can I see that Christ has power and authority in my life?"*

TAKE ACTION . . .

If you are fortunate enough to have a pastor, teacher, friend or relative with whom you can "really level," discuss these questions together: "Just how totally committed are we to Jesus Christ? What evidences of our commitment do we see in our lives, in our everyday practices and actions? How can we strengthen and increase this commitment? What can we actually do or say?"

Continue the experiments suggested in "Take Action . . ." for chapter 2. For example, why not try verbalizing the Gospel to your parents? If they are Christians too, this experiment could be of value in helping you see their point of view on Christ and vice versa. If they are not Christians, this kind of an approach could be a way to witness to them without a lot of tension and ill feelings.

*These ideas adapted from *How to Give Away Your Faith,* Paul Little, Inter-Varsity Press, pp. 15,16.

CHAPTER 4

How do you get to know Christ?

Kicked out of his parents' home while he was still in high school, Angelo tried living in an apartment with three other guys, but eventually two of them were drafted and the other one went back home and he was out in the street with no job and no money ... and no place to stay.

Because Angelo loved to surf he thought he'd try sleeping on the sand in a small cave on the beach near San Diego, Calif. A few days stretched into a few weeks and for a while it was kicks. With his guitar, his surfboard and a few clothes, he had all he needed. He made a little money by going up to groups of people on the beach and playing folk songs (charge, 50c).

But eventually, winter came and there weren't many groups on the beach. Finally, Angelo ran completely out of money and had to sell his guitar to buy food.

A few days later he was walking along the beach

collecting driftwood for a fire and he saw a group of around 30 teen-agers and some adults gathered around a roaring fire. It turned out to be some high schoolers from a church in El Cajon (suburb of San Diego) having their annual winter beach party. They invited him to stop and get warm by the fire and have something to eat and he did.

Angelo also stayed on to hear a short talk by the director of the group who talked about hope being a wish, and that the hope within this group of church kids was in Jesus Christ. He didn't get it, but he did have to admit these kids did seem to be on top of life.

He started away from the fire and the leader stopped him and asked him to talk. As they sat on a sea wall and watched a game of volley ball among some of the church kids, this guy mentioned the physical laws that governed the ball like the law of gravity. Then he started talking about spiritual laws and about God having a plan for his life.

This youth leader mentioned the idea that man is sinful and God is holy. Angelo certainly agreed with that. Then they also talked about this gap between God and man and that Jesus Christ, God's Son, had spanned the gap. Would he like to accept Jesus Christ as his own Saviour? Sure, why not, but how do you do that? By prayer, said the youth leader, and so they prayed and by faith Angelo asked Christ to come into his life.

The youth leader said he'd be back the next night to pick him up and take him to a youth meeting at his church. The next night it looked like the youth leader wasn't coming, but he finally showed up a half an hour late and they went to the meeting. On the way they stopped for hamburgers and Angelo didn't have any trouble putting several away. They were very friendly at the church and the pastor invited him to stay in a house trailer on the church grounds. Next morning Angelo mentioned to the pastor's wife that it was nice to sleep with covers for a change. (The only "covers" in the cave at the beach was the sand that he would burrow into behind a makeshift windbreak made out of his surfboard.)

Did the "decision for Christ" really stick? Two weeks later the writer for a national youth magazine talked to Angelo and learned that he was ready to take anything God had to offer and that God had already provided him with a job in a hospital—and a place to stay too.

And how did he feel about being a Christian? Angelo smiled from ear to ear and said "I have no regrets . . . I only wish everyone had this hope."*

This kind of story just doesn't happen too often. But it has certain resemblances to a story in John's Gospel. A man who was searching for real answers in life found them one night when he talked to another Man and learned that he had to be "born again." "Born again? What kind of talk is that?" Read on and see for yourself. Just as there is only one way to be born into this life, there is only one way to be "born again"—and the second birth is far more important than even the first . . .

*This incident really happened. It is reported in the February 1967 issue of *Campus Life*. The surfer's name is Dave Spry (nickname Angelo). He was led to Christ by Stan McNeil, youth director of a church in a San Diego suburb at that time.

John 3:1-21

[1,2]After dark one night a Jewish religious leader named Nicodemus, a member of the sect of the Pharisees, came for an interview with Jesus. "Sir," he said, "we all know that God has sent You to teach us. Your miracles are proof enough of this."

[3]Jesus replied, "With all the earnestness I possess I tell you this: Unless you are born again, you can never get into the Kingdom of God."

["Born again!" exclaimed Nicodemus. "What do You mean? How can an old man go back into his mother's womb and be born again?"

[5]Jesus replied, "What I am telling you so earnestly is this: Unless one is born of water[q] and the Spirit, he cannot enter the Kingdom of God. [6]Men can only reproduce human life, but the Holy Spirit gives new life from heaven; [7]So don't be surprised at My statement that you must be born again! [8]Just as you can hear the wind but can't tell where it comes from or where it will go next, so it is with the Spirit. We do not know on whom He will next bestow this life from heaven."

[9]"What do You mean?" Nicodemus asked.

[10,11]Jesus replied, "You, a respected Jewish teacher, and yet you don't understand these things? I am telling you what I know and have seen—and yet you won't believe Me. [12]But if you don't even believe Me when

33

I tell you about such things as these that happen here among men, how can you possibly believe if I tell you what is going on in heaven? ¹³For only I, the Man of Heaven,^r have come to earth and will return to heaven again. ¹⁴And as Moses in the wilderness lifted up the bronze image of a serpent on a pole, even so must I be lifted up upon a pole, ¹⁵So that anyone who believes in Me will have eternal life.

¹⁶For God loved the world so much that He gave His only Son so that anyone who believes in Him shall not perish but have eternal life. ¹⁷God did not send His Son into the world to condemn the world, but to save it. ¹⁸There is no eternal doom awaiting those who trust Him to save them. But those who don't trust Him have already been tried and condemned for not believing in the only^s Son of God. ¹⁹Their sentence is based on this fact: that the Light from heaven came into the world, but they loved the darkness more than the Light, for their deeds were evil. ²⁰They hated the heavenly Light because they wanted to sin in the darkness. They stayed away from that Light for fear their sins would be exposed and they would be punished. ²¹But those doing right come gladly to the Light to let everyone see that they are doing what God wants them to."

Bronze serpent reference predicts Christ's death

In the episode of Moses and the bronze serpent (Num. 21:5-9) there is a picture of God offering forgiveness to the man who repents of his sin. Because of their murmuring against Moses and God, the Israelites deserved punishment, and poisonous snakes came among them to deal out that punishment. But when the people came to Moses and admitted their sin and expressed their sorrow for it, Moses prayed to God for the people and God revealed to him the method of salvation from the fiery serpents: Make a bronze serpent and raise it up on a pole. Anyone bitten by a fiery serpent could look to this bronze serpent in repentance and faith and he would not die. Jesus is saying in v. 14 that just as in the incident of the bronze serpent, there would be another time when He (Jesus) would be lifted up on a pole (the cross) to die for man's sins. Anyone who believes in Him and His death on the cross to pay for man's sins will have eternal life.

The wind is still blowing

All in all, it must have been a rather startling evening for Nicodemus. He started out to have a stimulating conversation with another human being whom he thought was a great teacher or prophet of some kind. He wound up eye to eye with God Himself. The interesting thing is that this kind of encounter still happens today. The wind is still blowing. The Holy Spirit is still at work. For example, here are the personal reports of young men and women who have experienced what it means to be "born again" . . .

Eddie Waxer, Michigan State University—Have you ever become lost in the deep woods and feared that you may never find your way out? This was just the feeling which possessed me for most of my life. I wanted very much to lead a good life, but my human controls were never capable of achieving it.

My background is Judaism. At age 13 I had my Bar Mitzvah, the religious ritual in which a Jewish boy becomes a man. I did not find peace or satisfaction in rituals, and I rejected all religion.

During spring vacation of my sophomore year at Michigan State I met a girl who was very attractive, very intelligent, and a fine tennis player. One night after tennis we talked about Jesus Christ. She was the first person of my own age whom I had ever met who talked about Jesus Christ as if she knew Him. I was amazed that such a sharp girl held such beliefs.

One night soon after, I knelt in prayer and opened my heart asking Jesus to come in. The following morning, I woke up happy for a change, and some of the fellows on my floor remarked about it. I had a new enthusiasm and interest for life that I had never known before.*

Bill Hosmer, University of California—After one year at Cal and a near nervous breakdown, I found my life totally

*From "Collegians Speak," *Collegiate Challenge*, March 1963, p. 10.

without purpose. Knowing I would never find the answer in textbooks, I decided not to return to school my junior year until I had what I was looking for.

That next fall, I began hitchhiking my way north to "find myself." After several months and thousands of miles, I was no closer to my goal than when I had started. In addition, no one I talked to had the answer and many were themselves actively searching. In complete defeat I returned to Cal in February of 1964.

Shortly thereafter a Campus Crusade for Christ team spoke in my fraternity. They quoted Jesus Christ as saying, "I am the Way, the Truth, and the Life; no man comes to the Father but by Me." I realized that I had to make a decision for Christ. I talked to Christians and saw they had something that I didn't have. In the Gospel of John, I found that if Christ really was who He claimed to be, He would come into my life if I invited Him to do so.

I did invite Jesus Christ into my life. He has made a fantastic difference. Outwardly, friends have noticed my new purpose and positive attitude about life. Inwardly, I have a new depth of understanding of God and the Bible. In Christ I have found the truth and meaning for life for which I have searched so intensely.*

Lana Yong, University of California—Most people are either looking for or have found a purpose in life. My great dream was to make a significant contribution in the world of science. I succeeded in my own eyes when, at 18, I won first place in the California Science Fair with a project designed to save human lives. But still I was miserable. My self-made goals proved insufficient for my own happiness. That night I even considered jumping from my 14-story hotel window, but cried myself to sleep instead.

I lost interest in knowledge and education, but enrolled as a status-seeker at UC. I met some students in Campus Crusade for Christ and discovered that God loved me and had a wonderful plan for my life. These friends lived with a fullness and quality of life that I did not possess. I had been taught to fear God and ignorance prevented me from knowing Him. Later, a staff member of Campus Crusade shared with me how I could know Christ and experience His love and plan for me. I recognized my need for Him as

*From "Collegians Speak about Meaning in Life," *Collegiate Challenge*, October, 1965, p. 12.

my Saviour and Lord, and in prayer that day I gave my life to Him.

Jesus Christ has given me eternal life with *infinite* meaning and purpose. Now I am experiencing His love and plan and I no longer fear God. Nor do I wonder about the future—I have one!*

When you deal with the top . . .

John 3:16 is possibly the most famous verse in the Bible. It is the "mini-Gospel," a capsule statement on just what Christianity is all about. But don't overlook the verse that follows because it carries an important thought that some people sometimes overlook. Christianity is not another "religion" in which men can seek to find God, discover peace of mind, achieve spiritual tranquility, etc. Christianity offers the only solution to man's basic problem of sin. If you grant that Christ is God Himself, then it follows that in Christ and in Christ only will you find salvation and eternal life. As John puts it, "God did not send His Son into the world to condemn the world, but to save it."

But John minces no words in his next few lines. In vs. 18-21 he makes it clear that Christ is not just "one more way to God." He is "the Way" and if you will not have Him as Saviour, you must take Him as judge. There is no third choice because Christ is God Himself, not some human type of Saviour, not some great religious leader, not some great teacher. He is—God *Himself!* When you deal with the top there is no higher place to go.

A dean of students in a major university in Oregon discovered what it meant to "deal with the top" when

*From "Collegians Speak about Meaning in Life," *Collegiate Challenge,* January, 1965, p. 11.

37

**WHEN YOU DEAL WITH THE TOP,
THERE IS NO HIGHER PLACE TO LOOK**

he tried to advise college men who had academic or personal problems. He soon saw that he had not solved many of these same problems in his own life.

Then this dean became advisor to a group of students who met regularly on campus for Bible study and prayer. Through his experience with this group, the dean saw that he had to re-evaluate his entire concept of Christianity. He discovered that faith does not come in an organizational membership, but in a relationship to the Lord Jesus Christ. He began reading the Bible and the great message of the Gospel started making sense.

In the dean's own words, "I saw that for 31 years, I had lived for self. I decided I wanted to live the rest of my life for Jesus Christ alone. I asked God to forgive me and to make my life His own. I was assured by God's Word that, 'If any man be in Christ, he is a new creature: old things are passed away; behold all things become new'" (II Cor. 5:17).

Oh yes, the dean's name—Mark Hatfield, former

Governor of Oregon who went on to be a United States Senator.*

John 3:22-36

²²Afterwards Jesus and His disciples left Jerusalem and stayed for a while in Judea and baptized there. ²³,²⁴At this time John the Baptist was not yet in prison. He was baptizing at Aenon, near Salim, because there was plenty of water there.

²⁵One day someone began an argument with John's disciples, telling them that Jesus' baptism was best.ᵗ ²⁶So they came to John and said, "Master, the man you met on the other side of the Jordan River—the one you said was the Messiah—He is baptizing too, and everybody is going over there instead of coming here to us."

²⁷John replied, "God in heaven appoints each man's work. ²⁸My work is to prepare the way for that man so that everyone will go to Him. You yourselves know how plainly I told you that I am not the Messiah. I am here to prepare the way before Him—that is all. ²⁹The crowds will naturally go to the main attraction"— the bride will go where the bridegroom is! A bridegroom's friends rejoice with him. I am the Bridegroom's friend, and I am filled with joy at His success. ³⁰He must become greater and greater, and I must become less and less.

³¹He has come from heaven and is greater than anyone else. I am of the earth, and my understanding is limited to the things of earth. ³²He tells what He has seen and heard, but how few believe what He tells them! ³³,³⁴Those who believe Him discover that God is a fountain of truth! For this one—sent by God— speaks God's words, for God's Spirit is upon Him without measure or limit. ³⁵The Father loves this man because He is His Son, and God has given Him everything there is. ³⁶And all who trust Him—God's Son—to

*Adapted from "Excellence: The Christian Standard," by Mark O. Hatfield, *Collegiate Challenge*, May 1965, pp. 6,7.

save them have eternal life; those who don't believe and obey Him shall never see heaven, but the wrath of God remains upon them."

Out—damned* spot

Here we have more of the same idea about Christ or judgment. This time it comes from John the Baptist, a man who made it his life's work to tell people that they should shape up because God Himself was coming into the world. As John points out in v. 36, we all deserve God's wrath because we all fall far short of His holy glory.

What we call "mistakes" He calls sin. What we call "asserting ourselves" He calls rebellion. What we call "self-respect" he calls arrogant pride. It's in all of us. Some of us cover it up better than others, but it's still there—just like the spot in Lady Macbeth's guilty palm.* The only way to get rid of that spot is to believe and trust in what God has done for us through His Son, Jesus Christ.

*From Shakespeare's *Macbeth*, Act V, Scene I, line 39. This allusion to Shakespeare's *Macbeth* is not meant as frivolous profanity. The spot (sin) is "damned" as John 3 clearly points out.

THE "SPOT" IS IN ALL OF US

TAKE TIME . . .

Use the following ideas to take time to take a second look at John 3 and apply it to your life and the daily situations that you face.

Wait until dark? Go back to John 2:23-25 and read straight through to John 3:2. Does Nicodemus' opening remark imply that he may have been one of those "curiosity seekers" to whom Jesus did not want to commit Himself? How would you have opened the conversation with Jesus in this situation?

The case of the banished birthright. Look again at John 3:3,4. Jesus ignores formalities and gets right to the point in an almost blunt way. Does Nicodemus get it when Christ talks about "being born again"? Why not? What would you have thought if Jesus had said this to you?

Flesh versus Spirit. Look again at John 3:5-7. Some commentators think that "born of water" seems to refer to normal processes that occur in every human birth. Others compare the water in v. 5 to the washing of regeneration in Titus 3:5. What is meant by the "washing of regeneration"? How is this part of the "new birth"?

The wind blows through communications gap. Does Nicodemus understand Jesus' illustration that real spiritual life is like the wind (John 3:8-12)? Remember that Nicodemus was a member of the religious establishment. Why would he be reluctant to accept the idea that the Holy Spirit brings life from heaven to anyone He chooses?

All it takes is a look. In John 3:13-15, Jesus makes Nicodemus aware that he is not simply talking philosophy with a "great teacher." What would your reaction be if someone told you that he was a "man of heaven"—that is, that he was divine? (For background on Jesus' reference to the bronze serpent, see Num. 21:8,9.)

The mini-Gospel. Compare John 3:16,17 with Rom. 5:8; I John 4:9; John 5:36,38; and I John 4:14. Then write down why John 3:16 is the Bible's "incomparable verse."

The choice is yours. Compare John 3:18-21 with I John 1:6. Can you walk in darkness (sin) and know the Light of the world (Jesus Christ)? What do these passages tell you about life's absolutely fundamental choice? Why is it the greatest choice of all?

TAKE INVENTORY . . .

If the old, old story in John 3 is fairly new to you, think through the choice that it offers. Is there any reason why you shouldn't make that choice right now?

If you've grown up in the church and in a Christian home, John 3:16 is undoubtedly "old hat" to you. Maybe that's just the trouble. Take another look at this "favorite memory verse." Think through—and for even better results, write down—why this verse is meaningful for your life. What is this verse really saying about God? About you? About your life?

If you feel quite sure that you have believed and trusted in Jesus Christ and have everlasting life, take inventory on the number of people with whom you have shared your faith. Do you find it easy or hard to tell others about Christ? What makes it hard? What could help you make it easier?

TAKE ACTION . . .

Share ideas about the Gospel from John 3 with a non-Christian this week. In order to take the pressure off and help you get started, tell this person that you are interested in other people's viewpoints on God and you would like to see how his viewpoints match up with yours. Point out that John 3 mentions that every man must be born again spiritually. The reason is that every man is in sin and needs the salvation offered in Jesus Christ. Emphasize that God loved the world so much that He gave His only Son in order to help man out of his hopeless dilemma of sin. Bring the person to a confrontation with Christ and let him see that the choice is darkness (sin) or light (Jesus Christ, God Himself).

If you want some other systems for presenting the Gospel, obtain a copy of "Have You Heard of the Four Spiritual Laws?" (Campus Crusade for Christ International, Arrowhead Springs, San Bernardino, Calif.) or the booklet "Becoming a Christian," John R. W. Stott, Inter-Varsity Press, 130 N. Wells Street, Chicago, Ill.

CHAPTER 5

How to be
a diplomatic witness

There was a certain barber who did a good job, was clean, fast, cheap, and he always gave a free sermon instead of trading stamps.

But what did one of his customers say—especially about the sermon? Did the barber lead him to the Lord with his fervent witnessing? Not exactly. That customer has been heard to say that he could believe in Jesus Christ if it weren't for that barber. This disgruntled customer can even remember many examples of how the barber has turned him off on Jesus Christ. There was the time, for instance, when this man walked into the barber shop, hung up his hat, and said in his most friendly voice ... "Hi, what's new?"

"Nothing," the barber replied, "except the good news that Christ died to save sinners and that sure includes you."

"That's new? You've been playing that line for me for ten years. Like a stuck record."

"Yeah, well the only thing new would be if you would listen to it for a change," said the barber, then he added ominously, "Beware lest thou forget the Lord."

"You can forget it as far as I'm concerned," retorted the man and he tried to switch the conversation to the weather, politics, anything. But the barber kept coming at him with Biblical bullets like these:

"We must all give an account before the judgment seat of Christ . . . the wicked shall be turned into hell ... how will you escape if you neglect so great a salvation?"

"Look," said the man, "if you care so much about my soul, where were you when I was in the hospital last month?"

"Well, I was busy. You know how my work keeps me tied down here."

"Yeah, you were too busy chasing the almighty dollar, that's what. I almost died, but did you come to talk to me? Uh-uh. You didn't care."

"Care? Of course, I care! Why I warned you over and over: 'It's appointed unto man once to die and after that the judgment!' "

"Sure, you've *told* me you care, but show me. Even I can tell the difference."

And so, that is why that man says today, "So

44

there—see why I'm not a Christian?"*

Yes, it's not too hard to see why this victim of a barber's razor-edged witness is not a Christian. Here is a definite example of witnessing without diplomacy. Is this the way Christ witnessed? In John 4 we watch Him in action. There is much the barber could learn from this message and much that we could learn as well . . .

John 4:1-42

1,2When the Lord knew that the Pharisees had heard about the greater crowds coming to Him than to John to be baptized and to become His disciples—(though Jesus Himself didn't baptize them, but His disciples did)—3He left Judea and returned to the province of Galilee. 4He had to go through Samaria on the way, 5,6And around noon as He approached the village of Sychar, He came to Jacob's Well, located on the parcel of ground Jacob gave to his son Joseph. Jesus was tired from the long walk in the hot sun and sat wearily beside the well. 7Soon a Samaritan woman came to draw water, and Jesus asked her for a drink.

8He was alone at the time as His disciples had gone into the village to buy some food. 9The woman was surprised that a Jew would ask a "despised Samaritan" for anything—usually they wouldn't even speak to them! —and she remarked about this to Jesus.

10He replied, "If you only knew what a wonderful gift God has for you, and who I am, you would ask Me for some *living* water!"

11"But you don't have a rope or a bucket," she said, "and this is a very deep well! From where would you get this living water? 12And besides, are you greater than our ancestor Jacob? How can you offer better water than this which he and his sons and cattle enjoyed?"

*Adapted from "Are They Getting the Message?" by Dr. David Augsburger, *Eternity*, February, 1968, p. 12.

45

¹³Jesus replied that people soon became thirsty again after drinking this water. ¹⁴"But the water I give them," He said, "becomes a perpetual spring within them, watering them forever with eternal life."

¹⁵"Please, sir," the woman said, "give me some of that water! Then I'll never be thirsty again and won't have to make this long trip out here every day."

¹⁶"Go and get your husband," Jesus told her.

¹⁷"But I'm not married," the woman replied.

"All too true!" Jesus said. ¹⁸"For you have had five husbands, and you aren't even married to the man you're living with now! [You couldn't have spoken a truer word!"ᵛ]

¹⁹"Sir," the woman said, "You must be a prophet! ²⁰But say, tell me, why is it that you Jews insist that Jerusalem is the only place of worship, while we Samaritans claim it is here [at Mount Gerazimᵂ,] where our ancestors worshiped?"

²¹⁻²⁴Jesus replied, "The time is coming, Ma'am, when we will no longer be concerned about whether to wor-

---

Why the Jews and Samaritans hated each other

In this episode, Jesus and His disciples were passing through "enemy territory." In Jesus' time, there were three sections to Palestine: Judea in the south, Samaria in the middle, and Galilee in the north. Samaria was inhabited by "half-breed" Jews who had inter-married with people from the conquering Assyrians some 500 years before. Inter-marriage (strictly forbidden among Jews) was bad enough, but these Samaritan "turncoats" had then further deepened the rift between themselves and the "pure-blood" Jews when they tried to sabotage the rebuilding of Jerusalem under Ezra and Nehemiah around 450 to 400 B.C. Jesus was considered to be a Rabbi (teacher) and He completely broke tradition when He met the Samaritan woman and asked her for a drink. In addition, it was unheard of for a Jewish man—especially a Rabbi—to speak to a woman, particularly a Samaritan woman. In fact, some of the Pharisees were known as the "bruised and bleeding Pharisees" because they would shut their eyes whenever they saw a woman on the street and walked into walls, etc., by accident. For more on this, see the **Gospel of John, Vol. 1,** translated and interpreted by William Barclay, Published by the Saint Andrew Press, Edinburgh, 1956; and in USA by the Westminster Press, 1958, pp. 142,143.

ship the Father here or in Jerusalem! For it's not *where* we worship that counts, but *how* we worship—is our worship spiritual and real? Do we have the Holy Spirit's help? For God is Spirit, and we must have His Spirit's help to worship as we should. The Father wants this kind of worship from us. But you Samaritans know so little about Him, worshiping blindly, while we Jews know all about Him, for salvation comes to the world through the Jews."

²⁵The woman said, "Well, at least I know that the Messiah will come—the one they call Christ—and when He does, He will explain everything to us."

²⁶Then Jesus told her, "I am the Messiah!"

²⁷Just then His disciples arrived. They were surprised to find Him talking to a woman, but none of them asked Him why, or what they had been discussing. ²⁸Then the woman left her waterpot beside the well and went back to the village and told everyone, ²⁹"Come and meet a man who told me everything I ever did! Can this be the Messiah?" ³⁰So the people came streaming from the village to see Him.

³¹Meanwhile, the disciples were urging Jesus to eat.

³²"No," He said, "I have some food you don't know about!"

³³"Who brought it to Him?" the disciples asked each other.

³⁴Then Jesus explained: "My nourishment comes from doing the will of God who sent Me and from finishing His work. ³⁵Do you think the work of harvesting will not begin until the summer ends four months from now? Look around you! Vast fields of human souls are ripening all around us and are ready now for reaping. ³⁶The reapers will be paid good wages and will be gathering eternal souls into the granaries of heaven! What joys await the sower and the reaper, both together! ³⁷For it is true that one sows and someone else reaps. ³⁸I sent you to reap where you didn't sow; others did the work, and you received the harvest!"

³⁹Many from that Samaritan village believed He was

the Messiah because of the woman's report: "He told me everything I ever did!" [40](When they came out to see Him at the well, they begged Him to stay at their village; and He did, for two days, [41]long enough for many of them to believe in Him after hearing Him. [42]Then they said to the woman, "Now we believe because we have heard Him ourselves, not just because of what you told us. He is indeed the Saviour of the world.")

Seven principles for diplomatic witnessing

As He talks with the woman at the well, Christ demonstrates at least seven sound principles for witnessing effectively.* The Bible-spouting barber whom you met earlier in this chapter violates almost every one, as you will see . . .

1. *You have to contact others socially.* In other words, to go fishing you go where the fish are. Too many Christians think they "have to get people to come to church" in order to witness to them. Actually, the only way you would catch certain people in church would be dead, but they would listen to someone talk about Christ on the street, in a car, in a restaurant booth, etc., etc., etc.

You will have to give the barber credit. He was certainly willing to talk to people outside of church. In fact, he tried to turn his barber shop into a rescue mission. His listeners, however, didn't seem to appreciate his efforts to save them. If you take a look at the other six principles in John 4 you can get an idea why.

*These seven principles are adapted from chapter 2 "How to Witness" in *How to Give Away Your Faith*, Paul Little, Inter-varsity Press, 1966. For excerpts from this chapter see Appendix in this book, p. 222.

2. *Establish a common interest.* Note that Jesus doesn't open the conversation with something like, "Lady, don't you know I am the Messiah and that you should believe in Me?" Instead He starts with something she is thinking about —namely, water. He lays a simple foundation on which to build the conversation.

Too many Christians neglect this vital principle when they try to "witness." Instead of establishing common ground or instead of leading up to a logical reference to spiritual things, many would-be Christian witnesses attack in the same way that the barber did. They shoot from the hip with a fusillade of Biblical bullets that leaves the victim "shot down" or running for psychological cover.

3. *Arouse curiosity.* Jesus moved from talking about well water to "living water." When He did this,

ARE YOU AFRAID TO CONTACT NON-CHRISTIANS SOCIALLY?

ALL HAVE SINNED AND COME SHORT... *REPENT* AND BE BAPTIZED... YOU MUST BE BORN AGAIN... BELIEVE IN CHRIST AND YOU SHALL BE SAVED...

DO YOU FAIL TO ESTABLISH A COMMON INTEREST?

REPENT

REPENT! THE END DRAWS NIGH... I'M A CHRISTIAN... ASK ME!

DO YOU CAUSE CURIOSITY OR DISGUST?

Jesus "threw out the bait" and the Samaritan woman took it.

Perhaps Christians need to spend less time learning how to become "fishers of men" and more time learning how to be "baiters of hooks." The barber, of course, would never bother with baiting a hook. He much preferred to harpoon his victims before they had a chance to get comfortably settled in his chair.

4. *Don't rush things.* In vs. 10-12 you get a clear impression that Christ has definitely aroused the woman's curiosity. In vs. 13-15 we watch Him as He continues to let the conversation proceed at her rate of speed, not His. At the same time, He continues to make her even more curious and more interested.

Jesus doesn't rattle off a string of proof-texts or give her the plan of the kingdom of God in a basic outline. The barber, on the other hand, opened his "witnessing" with a burst of Bible fire and he never let up. In other words, the barber "went too far" the first time he opened his mouth.

5. *Cultivate, don't condemn.* In vs. 16-19 we watch Jesus point the woman to a real need without condemning her. With supernatural insight, Jesus detected the woman's adultery and wholesale failure in five marriages. But, He didn't inform her that she was a "dirty sinner." She already knew that. She didn't need sermons, she needed assistance.

When they try to witness, Christians often unwittingly condemn people in subtle (and sometimes not so subtle) ways. For example, a Christian may refuse a drink or a cigarette by saying, "No thanks, I'm a Christian." The result, of course, is that the listener immediately equates Christianity with not drinking or smoking, and to him this means Christianity is nothing more than some kind of rigid and negative code.

In the barber's case, he condemned his customer with his opening remark by telling him that Christ died to save sinners, and that sure included him. This kind of cliché convinces few people of their sin. Instead, it clouds the issue and causes many people to think that Christianity is some sort of refuge for "holier than thou" fanatics.

6. *Don't get sidetracked with secondary issues.* In vs. 20-24 we see how Jesus keeps the conversation on course instead of getting into a pointless argument about "the proper place to worship." Jesus stays right on the sub-

WAIT! STOP! I WANT YOU TO SIGN THIS DECISION SLIP NOW!

DO YOU SOMETIMES GO TOO FAR WITH FRAGILE PROSPECTS?

SORRY, I DON'T SMOKE. I'M A CHRISTIAN, YOU KNOW.

DO YOU CONDEMN PEOPLE OR CULTIVATE THEM?

I CAN'T REALLY AGREE WITH YOU THAT CHRISTIANITY IS UNFAIR BECAUSE IT SAYS ALL THE PAGANS ARE GOING TO HELL. FOR EXAMPLE,

DO YOU STICK TO THE POINT OR STRAY OFF ON TANGENTS?

ject of spirituality by pointing out that it's not where a person worships, but how (vs. 23,24).

Many people try to dodge the real issue with various stock arguments: "Well, I could never go to your church because you are against drinking and smoking." Another popular dodge is to bring up the old question about "are the heathen really lost?" and accuse Christianity of being unfair because it supposedly says all the Hottentots are going to hell.

Many of these sideroads are used by people in an attempt to get the course of the conversation off of themselves and their basic need of a personal relationship to Jesus Christ.

How does the Christian guide the conversation back to the main highway? Well, he certainly doesn't use the barber's approach. In a way, the barber never got the conversation going in the right direction in the first place. The barber's best weapon was the quoting of the Bible. But as he quoted Scripture, he manhandled it instead of allowing the Holy Spirit to use it. There are many opportunities for use of Scripture when witnessing to someone else, but it should be used as a light to illuminate the truth, not as a club to "clobber a sinner."

7. *Bring your listener face to face with Jesus Christ.* Jesus could have opened His conversation with the woman at the well by saying, "Lady, I am the Messiah. I have you pegged." If He had done so, the woman probably would have written Him off as some kind of religious nut.

Instead, Jesus quietly and steadily brought the woman along to the real issue: What would she do with Christ Himself? (See v. 26.) This final step is

DO YOU CUT THROUGH THE 'SMOKE-SCREEN TO
CONFRONT THEM WITH CHRIST?

often the most difficult. However, unless you bring
your listener to a direct confrontation with Jesus
Christ and His claims (not your claims or interpretations), you have not witnessed. You have only
wandered through conversational bypath meadows,
and in so doing, you can wind up leading people,
not to Christ, but astray.

The entire account of the barber's witness to his
disenchanted customer is a good example of never
bringing a person face to face with Jesus Christ. To
be sure, the barber used a lot of the Bible verses
and he mentioned Christ's name, but he did it in
such an obnoxious way that his customer never
really heard about Christ. He only heard the name
"Christ" used by a man who came through to him
as condemning and really unconcerned about him
personally. In other words, the man reacted to the
barber by thinking, "If this is Christianity, I want
no part of it." The barber was communicating all

right, but the message of salvation that he thought he was delivering just wasn't coming through because *he* wasn't coming through.

In the mid-1960's a communications expert named Marshall McLuhan came out with a theory that communication does not depend basically on the message being sent, but real communication depends more on the medium (the means or way) used for sending that message. One of McLuhan's famous slogans became a byword: "The medium is the message."*

Now in the case of the barber, the "medium" was the barber himself, and that was the only "message" that his customer was getting. All the man could hear was the preachy babbling of someone who obviously wasn't really personally concerned about him.

In the 4th chapter of John, however, we see a perfect example of the flawless blending of the "medium" and the "message." Christ is the message that the Christian wants to communicate. And, in this chapter we see that Christ is also a most effective medium of communication. His witness was "diplomatic" not because He used some clever psychological rules, but because He cared about the woman and was interested in her personally.

And what happened? The woman, in turn, ran back to town and it was a case of the "medium becoming the message" all over again. She quickly told her neighbors what had happened to her and they flocked to "see for themselves." The woman

*See *The Medium Is the Massage,* Marshall McLuhan, (New York: Random House, Inc., 1967).

was an effective means of communicating Christ to her neighbors because she was excited and involved in telling them about what had happened to her. As a result, people took time to be confronted squarely with the claims of Christ on their lives. The result was that they, too, believed and recognized Him as the Saviour of the world.

John 4:43-54

[43]At the end of the two days' stay He went on into Galilee.[x] [44]For as Jesus used to say, "A prophet is honored everywhere except in his own country!" [45]But the Galileans welcomed Him with open arms, for they had been in Jerusalem at the Passover celebration and had seen some of His miracles.[y] [46,47]In the course of His journey through Galilee He arrived at the town of Cana, where He had turned the water into wine. While He was there, a man in the city of Capernaum, whose son was very sick, heard that Jesus had come from Judea and was traveling in Galilee. This man went over to Cana, found Jesus, and begged Him to come to Capernaum with him and heal his son, who was now at death's door.

[48]Jesus asked, "Won't any of you believe in Me unless I do more and more miracles?"

[49]The official pled, "Sir, please come now before my child dies."

[50]Then Jesus told him, "Go back home. Your son is healed!"

And the man believed Jesus and started home.

[51]While he was on his way, some of his servants met him with the news that all was well—his son had recovered! [52]He asked them when the lad had begun to feel better, and they replied, "Yesterday afternoon at about one o'clock his fever suddenly disappeared!" [53]Then the father realized it was the same moment that Jesus had told him, "Your son is healed." And the of-

55

ficer and his entire household believed that Jesus was the Messiah. "This was Jesus' second miracle in Galilee after coming from Judea.

When nothing seems to happen . . .

These verses record Jesus' second miracle in Galilee. The first was the turning of water into wine at Cana. Now Jesus heals a government official's son without even going to his bedside. Various conclusions can be drawn from this incident, but perhaps the most useful observation for someone interested in "telling it like it is" is to note the official's faith. The man trusted Jesus— sight unseen, so to speak. This is frequently the very same situation for the Christian witness. He can only do and say so much and sometimes it doesn't look like anything is happening.

Perhaps that is the way it often seems for you. You hear stories about how people win others to Christ while on flights between Los Angeles and Chicago or they lead the cab driver to the Lord

before the meter passes $1.50. These incidents are wonderful examples of how God can work when He chooses, but the people *you* talk to don't seem to respond quite so easily. Perhaps all you can do is "believe and trust in Jesus," go on home and wait for God to work according to His will, not the "evangelistic" rule book.

TAKE TIME . . .

Use the following ideas to take time to take a second look at John 4 and apply it to your life and to any situations you face.

Starting with two strikes. Compare John 4:1-9; Luke 9:52,53; and John 8:48. Why is Jesus "starting with two strikes against Him" in this particular situation? Get a Bible dictionary or handbook from your church library and look up background on why the Jews and Samaritans hated each other. Also find data on the social stigma attached to a Jewish Rabbi talking to a woman.

Double talk leads to serious talk. Compare John 4:10-15 with Isa. 44:3; John 7:37-39; and Rev. 21:6. Who is the source of the "living water" that Jesus mentions? Why does Jesus talk in riddles that the Samaritan woman can't understand? What is Jesus trying to do?

Always stick to the point. Take another look at John 4:16-24 and compare with John 5:25 and Phil. 3:3. What is more important? Where you worship? Or what you worship? Write down some specific reasons for your answer.

A conversation brings confrontation. Review John 4:25,26 and compare with Matt. 26:63,64 and Mark 14:61,62. Go back through the first 26 verses of John 4 and analyze how Jesus brings the woman to this point. Why didn't He just start out by saying "Lady, I'm the Messiah. You should believe in me"?

He saw right through me! Look again at John 4:27-30 and match it up with John 7:26. When people have a genuine encounter with Christ, what should happen? What happens when a person comes face to face with God Himself? What is happening in your own experience?

Think "now"! Read John 4:31-38 again and compare John 4:37 and Micah 6:15 and Job 31:8. Can you think of times when you reaped (gained the benefit) because others had sown (done prior work)? When it comes to Christian witnessing which is more important, the sowing or the reaping? Why?

The best kind of "proof." Read John 4:39-42 and compare with I John 1:3 and John 9:25. What is the final step in the making of a Christian? Who helps a person take this final step?

TAKE INVENTORY . . .

Review the seven principles in this chapter (as well as the excerpts from *How to Give Away Your Faith* by Paul Little in the appendix, p. 222). Analyze your own efforts to witness for Christ according to these principles. Which principles do you need to use most often? Which principles have you been using without realizing it? Which principles seem most difficult to put into practice? Why are they difficult?

Think back to times when someone has "witnessed" to you and violated one or more of the principles outlined in John 4. Or think back to a time when you made an unsuccessful attempt to witness. Which of these principles did you fail to observe?

If your record in the game of witnessing is "O" wins, "O" losses, and "O" ties; try to analyze just why you have yet to take the field and how the seven principles in John 4 can help you play your first game.

TAKE ACTION . . .

Practice one or several of the basic principles outlined in John 4 this week. You might want to get together with a Christian friend and work on some of these points together. But also be praying about finding opportunities to use these principles when speaking to non-Christians.

Especially keep in mind principle three on arousing curiosity. Your prayer should be that the Holy Spirit would guide you to someone that He has been preparing. The way you'll find out is to "throw out the bait." Keep in mind however, that in throwing out the bait that you try to cast accurately and that you cast often enough.

CHAPTER 6

Why refuse to answer?

When opportunities come up to speak out for what you believe (more correctly for *Whom* you believe), do you say something, or do you often refuse to answer on the grounds ... that it might incriminate you? (Or is it that it would identify you?)

Here are a few examples ...

It's lunch time and you put your tray down on the table with the rest of the gang. You are about to dive in when you remember—grace! So you rub your eyes a few times with your fists, move your lips slightly, and hope that you have fulfilled your obligation unnoticed.

Just then, however, some wise guy yells, "Hey fellas, look at Holy Joe over there, praying yet. Say one for me, Joe."

Silence . . . and a slow simmer on your part. You will take their "persecution" like a martyr, you try to convince yourself. Deep in your heart, though, you know that this would be a terrific time to put in a plug for Christ, only you don't have the nerve.

Here's another. The phone rings. It's Dick inviting you to get together for a little picnic at which he casually mentions that there will be dancing at the Pavilion with plenty of beer. You could tell him why you don't feel you should go, but you don't want him to think you are a prude, so you make up a story about having another date that Saturday and suggest that he "call again sometime." The real reason for your refusal remains untold.

There are dozens of other instances that come up every day and every week. If you're in a group where somebody brings up Billy Graham and comments that he's always negative "preaching about sin and hell and that's what's wrong with the church anyway." You know that this person has it all wrong, but you don't say anything because it doesn't seem to be quite the right time or place.*

But is it ever "just the right time and just the right place"? In the next chapter of John, we find Jesus faced with misunderstanding, hatred, and ignorance. He gets in trouble with the religious authorities, and they roast Him plenty for breaking their rules. Is it "just the right time and just the right place" to stand up for the truth? Or is it time for Jesus to not worry about "convenience" and "tell it like it is?"

*Adapted from *Teen*, September 1, 1963, Harvest Publications, Chicago, Ill.

John 5:1-29

¹Afterwards Jesus returned to Jerusalem for one of the Jewish religious holidays. ²Inside the city near the Sheep Gate was Bethesda Pool, with five covered platforms or porches surrounding it. ³Crowds of sick folks —lame, blind, or with paralyzed limbs—lay on the platforms (waiting for a certain movement of the water, ⁴For an angel of the Lord came from time to time and disturbed the water, and the first person to step down into it afterwards was healed).ᶻ ⁵One of the men lying there had been sick for 38 years. ⁶When Jesus saw him and knew how long he had been ill, He asked him, "Would you like to get well?"

⁷"I can't," the sick man said, "for I have no one to help me into the pool at the movement of the water. While I am trying to get there, someone else always gets in ahead of me."

⁸Jesus told him, "Stand up, roll up your sleeping mat and go on home!"

⁹Instantly, the man was healed! He rolled up the mat and began walking!

But it was on the Sabbath when this miracle was done. ¹⁰So the Jewish leaders objected! They said to

---

Sabbath breaking: punishable by death!

All the concern by the Pharisees over Jesus' healing of the man on the Sabbath and then telling the man to carry his bed away might seem ridiculous today, but it was not ridiculous then. The Pharisees, a group that had tremendous influence over the people, believed a man could break the Sabbath by even carrying a needle in his robe or wearing shoes with nails in them (nails made the shoes a "burden"). For a man to carry his bed was a serious crime indeed, and the poor fellow probably wished he was lame again when the Jews reminded him of the actual words of their Sabbath law: "If anyone carries anything from a public place to a private house on the Sabbath intentionally, he is punishable by death by stoning."

—Adapted from **The Gospel of John, Volume 1.** Translated and interpreted by William Barclay. Published by the Saint Andrew Press, Edinburgh, 1956; and in USA by the Westminster Press, 1958. See pp. 178,179.

the man who was cured, "You can't work on the Sabbath! It's illegal to carry that sleeping mat!"

[11]"The man who healed me told me to," was his reply.

[12]"Who said such a thing as that?" they demanded.

[13]The man didn't know, and Jesus had disappeared into the crowd. [14]But afterwards Jesus found him in the Temple and told him, "Now you are well; don't sin as you did before,[a] or something even worse may happen to you."

[15]Then the man went to find the Jewish leaders, and told them it was Jesus who had healed him. [16]So they began harassing Jesus as a Sabbath breaker. [17]But Jesus replied, "My Father constantly does good,[b] and I'm following His example!"

[18]Then the Jewish leaders were all the more eager to kill Him because in addition to disobeying their Sabbath laws, He had spoken of God as His Father, thereby making Himself equal with God.

[19]Jesus replied, "The Son can do nothing by Himself. He does only what He sees the Father doing, and in the same way. [20]For the Father loves the Son, and tells Him everything He is doing; and the Son will do far more awesome miracles than this man's healing! [21]He will even raise from the dead anyone He wants to, just as the Father does. [22]And the Father leaves all judgment of sin to His Son, [23]So that everyone will honor the Son, just as they honor the Father. But if you refuse to honor God's Son, whom He sent to you, then you are certainly not honoring the Father. [24]I say emphatically that anyone who listens to My message and believes in God who sent Me has eternal life, and will never be damned for his sins, but has already passed out of death into life. [25]And I solemnly declare that the time is coming, in fact, it is here, when the dead shall hear My voice —the voice of the Son of God—and those who listen shall live. [26]The Father has life in Himself, and has granted His Son to have life in Himself, [27]And to judge the sins of all mankind because He is the Son of Man. [28]Don't

be so surprised! Indeed the time is coming when all the dead in their graves shall hear the voice of God's Son, [29]And shall rise again—those who have done good, to eternal life; and those who have continued in evil, to judgment.

Jesus signs His death warrant

Humanly speaking, Jesus is "signing His death warrant" as He clashes head-on with the religious prejudices of the Pharisees. He could have put off this encounter, but He chose to heal the man on the Sabbath and He chose to state emphatically just who He really was. Jesus counted the earthly cost involved in standing for heavenly things, and every Christian who has said that he "believes in Christ" should be able to say that he has done the same.

Take another look at John 5:24 and think about what it really means to "believe in Christ." Think it through. Do you believe in Christ just as many little children believe in Santa Claus? In other words, many little children believe that Santa Claus really exists (although, of course, he doesn't). Or perhaps you are like the Moslems, who believe that there once existed a Jesus who was a prophet of God. But as one Bible scholar has pointed out* John 5:24 might be better translated: "I say emphatically that anyone who listens to my message *and entrusts himself fully* to the God who sent Me has eternal life ..." Here is the key to being ready to give an answer for the hope that is in you. Do you simply believe certain doctrinal propositions that you have been taught, or have you entrusted yourself fully to Jesus Christ? It makes all the difference

*See "Unsaved Believers," Joseph Young, *His*, May 1965.

in the world—especially in a world that is often hostile to the Christian's ideas. It is in the hostile situations where the "trusters" are separated from the "believers."

John 5:30-38

[30]But I pass no judgment without consulting the Father. I judge as I am told. And My judgment is absolutely fair and just, for it is according to the will of God who sent Me and is not merely My own! [31]When I make claims about Myself they aren't believed, [32,33]But someone else, yes, John the Baptist,[e] is making these claims for Me too. You have gone out to listen to his preaching, and I can assure you that all he says about Me is true! [34]But the truest witness I have is not from a man, though I have reminded you about John's witness so that you will believe in Me and be saved. [35]John shone brightly for a while, and you benefited and rejoiced, [36]But I have a greater witness than John. I refer to the miracles I do; these have been assigned Me by the Father, and they prove that the Father has sent Me. [37]And the Father Himself has also testified about Me, though not appearing to you personally, or speaking to you directly.

[38]But you are not listening to Him, for you refuse to believe Me—the one sent to you with God's message. [39]You search the Scriptures, for you believe they give you eternal life. And the Scriptures point to Me! [40]Yet you won't come to Me so that I can give you this life eternal! [41,42]Your approval or disapproval means nothing to Me, for as I know so well, you don't have God's love within you. [43]I know, because I have come to you representing My Father and you refuse to welcome Me, though you readily enough receive those who aren't sent from Him, but represent only themselves! [44]No wonder you can't believe! For you gladly honor each other, but you don't care about the honor that comes from the only God! [45]Yet it is not I who will

accuse you of this to the Father—Moses will! Moses, on whose laws you set your hopes of heaven. "For you have refused to believe Moses. He wrote about Me, but you refuse to believe him, so you refuse to believe in Me. "And since you don't believe what he wrote, no wonder you don't believe Me either."

How to witness in a steel mill

There is a word that keeps popping up in this section of John 5. That word is "witness." Jesus mentions several "witnesses" to His deity—persons or writings that testify that He is indeed the Son of God. These witnesses include John the Baptist, the very miracles that Jesus has done, the Heavenly Father Himself, and the Holy Scriptures which were written about Christ. (See vs. 31-39.)

The Pharisees don't listen to Christ, of course, they cannot see the forest because they are too busy blazing their own particular trail through the trees. Actually, the Pharisees didn't really think they needed salvation. They much preferred their regulations and legalistic fine points to living in real fellowship with God.

But the point is, Jesus spoke up. He did not refuse to answer on the grounds that it might incriminate Him. In fact, He incriminated Himself quite thoroughly as far as the Pharisees were concerned.

But you may be thinking, "Well, that's fine for Jesus, but after all, He was the Son of God, so that gives Him a little bit of an edge, don't you think?"

Perhaps, but if to believe in Christ is to fully entrust yourself to Him, doesn't it follow that you also will have a "little bit of an edge"? That is, even though you may be afraid, if you step out in faith Christ will give you the courage and the power to do what you could never do alone.

Consider, for example, the story of a young fellow named Paul Freed, who worked in a steel mill where lunch hour consisted of card playing, dirty stories and the like.

Paul took the job one summer to make money for college. Among the thick-chested, brawny-armed steel men he felt like a skinny runt. It didn't seem to him that there was any way that he could communicate with men like this. And yet, as he sat eating his lunch and hearing dirty jokes and Jesus' name used only in vain, Paul often seemed to hear God saying, "Why don't you give these men a word of testimony?"

But Paul shrank from this idea. Teach Sunday School, yes. Give a testimony in church or at the young people's group or even on his own campus, yes ... but speak to these steel men? One of them might smash him like a bug.

Things came to a head one night as Paul found himself on a narrow catwalk a hundred feet above the tops of the roaring blast furnaces. A few nights before he had cut his leg badly on a rusty piece of wire and it had grown inflamed and infected. Now, as he crawled along the catwalk, the infected leg hit him and he suddenly felt sick and dizzy. Paul cried out to God for help, and it seemed as though God answered by saying, "Look, Paul, I didn't send you here to earn money or to work your way through college. I sent you here to be a witness for me."

Er...I don't know how to say this...

SOMETIMES IT'S HARD TO FIND A "CONVENIENT" TIME AND PLACE...

"Help me, Lord, and I promise you I'll be a witness for you in this mill," was his reply.

Somehow, Paul got to the end of the catwalk and that's all he remembered until he came to with several of the steel workers peering down on him. Two weeks in the hospital made him as good as new, although for awhile the doctors feared they would have to amputate his infected leg. He returned to the steel mill with three weeks left before the reopening of school and again found himself sitting around the circle at lunch time and remembering his promise that he would witness to the steel men.

Yes, he would witness, he would figure out a way to talk to them one by one. But instead, the Lord seemed to say, "No, do it now. Talk to them right now. They tell stories to each other and you have to listen, so why don't you tell them what I mean to you? You promised Me." Finally, with a shaking hand, Paul Freed reached into his pocket for his New Testament and said, "Men, I don't know how to say this. On my hospital bed I thought about all of you and when I was very sick I promised God I would tell you men about what He has done for me."

And then, as he read a few verses touching on the way to salvation and what Christ has done for all of us, Paul fully expected some of those meaty mill-fists to come slamming down on him to shut his mouth.

But that's not what happened. The men were strangely quiet and listened to every word. Afterward, one came up and said, "Boy, that took a lot of courage, what you did. I'd like to know more about Jesus. I've had a very miserable life. Everything has gone wrong. Would you tell me more about Jesus?"*

This story has a happy ending. The man who wanted to know more about Jesus accepted Christ as did many others before Paul returned to school. But even if the story didn't end so happily, here was an example of someone who didn't find the "convenient time and place" to speak for Christ. He made time and he spoke when it was hardly convenient.

Entrust yourself fully to God. He will give you that extra edge . . .

*Adapted from *Teen with a Future,* James R. Adair. Copyright 1965, Baker Book House. From an account by Paul E. Freed as told to Harry Albus.

TAKE TIME...

From healing to hostility. Read John 5:1-47 and try to get the entire incident in mind: Jesus heals a man and then is accused by the Jews of breaking their Sabbath law. Does Jesus admit that He has broken the law? To what authority does He appeal?

Do you want Christ in your life? Read John 5:1-9. Why did Jesus ask the man if he wanted to be healed? Do you think that, ultimately, Christ ever works in a person's life without invitation? Why?

The "law" closes in. Read John 5:10-16. What was the attitude of the Pharisees in this situation? What happens when you put rules and regulations ahead of genuine human need? In other words, was Jesus justified in breaking the "Sabbath laws" of the Pharisees? Did Jesus break the Sabbath law of His Father as recorded in the Ten Commandments? Give reasons for your answer.

A personal Christ or a God in a can? Read John 5:17-24. List different ways Jesus relates Himself with God. Follow the implications of what Jesus says to their logical conclusion. If Jesus were equal with God, what would this do to the Pharisees comfortable "legal establishment"? Why is it that you cannot have a personal relationship to Christ and an artificial, legalistic concept of God at the same time?

The "suspect" turns out to be the judge! Read John 5:25-30. If Jesus were only a man, how would you explain these words? If Jesus were God—one of the three Persons of the Trinity—why do these words make sense?

Evidence for the defense. Read John 5:31-36. Two "witnesses" for Christ's tremendous claims about Himself are named here. Which witness has more authority—John the Baptist or Jesus' miraculous works? How did the miracles of Christ complement the preaching of John the Baptist?

God put it in writing, but . . . Read John 5:37-47. What do these verses tell you about loving only the "letter of the law"? Can "love for the Bible" sometimes stand between a Christian and his love for Christ? How could this happen?

TAKE INVENTORY . . .

Think back to some "negative" situations that you have experienced when trying to witness for Christ. Why were they negative? What could you have done to be more positive? Analyze your own attitude. Was the situation basically negative because you were negative?

If you can't think back to any situations of any kind, this is the most negative condition of all. You are obviously afraid to say anything for Jesus Christ. Look back through John 5 and try to analyze why you are afraid. Do you feel you really know Christ personally? Is your belief in Him personal trust or simply mental assent to religious information?

TAKE ACTION . . .

Pray about a particularly difficult person that you have tried to witness to or that you have been thinking about approaching concerning spiritual things. As God leads you, try talking to that person this week and try using the principles Jesus shows in John 5. See if you can communicate to this person that you really do want to put love and concern for people above religious rules and regulations.

See if you can show him that you know where you stand with Jesus Christ. See if you can present evidence for your beliefs from Scripture. Above all, will you be close enough to Christ to let Him work through you? In the final analysis, an effective witness for Christ is not something that a Christian does, but it is something that a Christian allows Christ to do through him. This is a mystical idea that is hard to understand, but it is nonetheless a fact.

Keep in mind that as a Christian witness, you are not the message, you are the envelope that delivers the message. You are the "telephone line" over which the message is passed. If the line goes down or becomes snarled (if you grow cool on Christianity through your own neglect or selfishness), the message can't get through.

CHAPTER 7

Is the rat race worth it?

What is more important to you?

Things or people?

Accomplishment or character?

Being a "success" or living successfully?

Careful how you answer, because your deep visceral* feelings are the key to how effectively you will communicate Christ. If you're typical, you're in the pressure cooker labeled "You must get ahead in life." What's wrong with wanting to get ahead? Nothing—unless you put God behind, which is very easy to do.

For example, the push for grades in high schools and colleges has been so strong throughout the last decade that it's not unheard of for a serious student to put in 16 and 17 hours a day in classes, activities and homework. After four years of this in high

---

*A cruder (but perhaps more descriptive) term would be "gut-level."

school and four or more years of it in college you don't have a "success" ... you have a junior partner in "Ulcers Inc."

Grades aren't the only pressure. In many people there is the drive to be "Big Man on Campus." One fellow (a senior class president) got so sick of meeting standards and polishing his image that he started wishing that he could simply "do his best" and let it go at that. He finally escaped his own personal pressure cooker by realizing that God has given each of us certain abilities and that He accepts each of us just as we are. This class president finally learned to accept himself and his limitations and leave the rest of it with God.

And then, there was the girl whose high school years were a whirlwind of activities—meetings, plans, committees, fun, excitement, hard work— successville! This girl had little time for her family and less for God, and finally the pace began to tell. She began asking herself what she was really accomplishing and what she was doing that was of lasting value. Who would remember or care who designed the class float or had the lead in the class play? But her parents would remember when she couldn't take time to look at some slides of a family outing. Her little brother would remember the many times when she had failed to be a listening sister. God? Yes, God would not forget the many times she had been "too busy" to listen to Him.

This girl finally wised up and started re-evaluating her motives for her activities. She redirected her energies and began to feel free of needless pressure. She had more freedom to grow spiritually, more

YOU NEVER WIN THE RAT RACE...
YOU ONLY RUN IT

time to spend being directed by God. She became consciously aware of why she was doing something, and the more she stopped to ask herself this question the more fulfillment she got out of life.*

The examples can go on and on. But as far as telling it like it is about Jesus Christ, the basic question is, "Will seeking success spoil Joe Christian?" The answer is yes, if that's all he is really seeking. Jesus had to get this point across to a huge crowd one day—a crowd that thought that He could win their war on poverty and their struggle against Roman oppression all in one week or less. Watch Jesus in action as He throws away popularity and apparent "success" in order to teach a basic

---

*The cases of the senior class president and the girl who got "gobbled up" by activities are adapted from true accounts as told by Jim Whitmar and Marilou West in "My World the Pressure Cooker," Dean Merrill, *Campus Life*, February 1968.

truth: those who truly want to follow and communicate Him are not interested in "success." They have even greater goals in mind ...

John 6:1-25

[1]After this, Jesus crossed over the Sea of Galilee, also known as the Sea of Tiberias. [2-5]And a huge crowd many of them pilgrims on their way to Jerusalem for the annual Passover celebration,[d] were following Him wherever He went, to watch Him heal the sick. So when Jesus went up into the hills and sat down with His disciples around Him, He soon saw a great multitude of people climbing the hill, looking for Him. Turning to Philip He asked, "Philip, where can we buy bread to feed all these people?" [6](He was testing Philip, for He already knew what He was going to do!)

[7]Philip replied, "It would take a fortune[e] to begin to do it!"

[8,9]Then Andrew, Simon Peter's brother, spoke up. "There's a youngster here with five barley loaves and a couple of fish! But what good is that with all this mob?"

[10]"Tell everyone to sit down," Jesus ordered. And all of them—the approximate count of the men only was 5,000—sat down on the grassy slopes. [11]Then Jesus took the loaves and gave thanks to God and passed them out to the people. Afterwards He did the same with the fish. And everyone ate until full. [12]"Now gather the scraps," Jesus told His disciples, "so that nothing is wasted."

[13]And 12 baskets were filled with the leftovers! [14]When the people realized what a great miracle had happened, they exclaimed, "Surely, He is the Prophet we have been expecting!"

[15]Jesus saw that they were ready to take Him by force and make Him their king, so He went higher into the mountains alone.

[16]That evening His disciples went down to the shore to wait for Him. [17]But as darkness fell and Jesus still

hadn't come back, they got into the boat and headed across the lake toward Capernaum. [18,19]But soon a gale swept down upon them as they rowed, and the sea grew very rough. They were three or four miles out when suddenly they saw Jesus walking toward the boat! They were terrified, [20]But He called out to them and told them not to be afraid.

[21]Then they were willing to let Him in, and immediately the boat was where they were going![f]

[22,23]The next morning, back across the lake, crowds began gathering on the shore [waiting to see Jesus[g]]. For they knew that He and His disciples had come over together and that the disciples had gone off in their boat, leaving Him behind. Several small boats from Tiberias were nearby, [24]So when the people saw that Jesus wasn't there, or His disciples, they got into the boats and went across to Capernaum to look for Him. [25]When they arrived and found Him, they said, "Sir, how did You get here?"

A favorite son candidate?

The feeding of the 5000 is the first miracle that Jesus performs in front of a crowd of any size and the effect is interesting. The Jewish citizens, who had been living under Roman occupation for many years, began to calculate just what this fellow Jesus could do for them. If He could solve a food problem for 5000 people, could He not also defeat the Roman legions in battle with a miraculous wave of His little finger? Here indeed seemed a way of harnessing the power of God for their own ends.

The people began talking excitedly about drafting the Nazarene carpenter to be their "King." The situation immediately turned into a "political convention." Ironically, it was a convention where all the delegates were thoroughly convinced about who their candidate should be except one—the candidate Himself. Jesus tried to slip away, but the crowd followed Him to Capernaum and the very next day—in the synagogue—He again faced their wildly enthusiastic offer to become their King. Success seemed within Jesus' grasp. All He had to do was step forward and make His acceptance speech...

John 6:26-58

[26]Jesus replied, "The truth of the matter is that you want to be with Me because I fed you, not because you believe in Me. [27]But you shouldn't be so concerned about perishable things like food. No, spend your energy seeking the eternal life that I the Man from Heaven[h] can give you. For God the Father has sent Me for this very purpose."

[28]They replied, "What should we do to satisfy God?"

[29]Jesus told them, "This is the will of God, that you believe in the one He has sent."

[30,31]They replied, "You must show us more miracles if You want us to believe You are the Messiah. Give us free bread every day, like our fathers had while they journeyed through the wilderness! As the Scriptures say, 'Moses gave them bread from heaven.' "

[32]Jesus said, "Moses didn't give it to them! My Father did.[i] And now He offers you true Bread from heaven. [33]The true Bread is a Person—the one sent by God from heaven, and He gives life to the world."

[34]"Sir," they said, "give us that bread every day of our lives!"

[35]Jesus replied, "I am the Bread of Life! No one coming to Me will ever be hungry again! Those believing in Me will never thirst! [36]But the trouble is, as I have told you before, you haven't believed even though you have seen Me. [37]But some will come to Me—those the Father has given Me—and I will never, never reject them. [38]For I have come here from heaven to do the will of God who sent Me, not to have My own way!

76

[39]And this is the will of God, that I should not lose even one of all those He has given Me, but that I should raise them to eternal life at the Last Day! [40]For it is My Father's will that everyone who sees His Son and believes on Him should have eternal life, and that I should raise him at the Last Day."

[41]Then the Jews began to murmur against Him because He claimed to be the Bread from heaven. [42]"What?" they exclaimed. "Why, he is merely Jesus, the son of Joseph, whose father and mother we know. What is this he is saying, that he came down from heaven?"

[43]But Jesus replied, "Don't murmur among yourselves about My saying that. [44]For no one can come to Me unless the Father who sent Me draws him to Me, and at the Last Day I will bring them all back to life. [45]As it is written in the Scriptures, 'They shall all be taught of God.'

"Those the Father speaks to, who learn the truth from Him, will be attracted to Me. [46](Not that anyone actually sees the Father, for only I have seen Him.) [47]How earnestly I tell you this—anyone who believes in Me already has eternal life! [48]Yes, I am the Bread of

---

The bread of life is for "hidden hunger"

When Jesus calls Himself the "Bread of Life" He is saying that He can satisfy the "hidden hunger" that comes when a person is not at peace with God and properly related to Him. But the Jews were so materialistically minded, that they actually thought that Jesus was suggesting cannibalism (v. 52) and they were further abhorred when He mentioned "drinking His blood" (vs. 53-56). To drink blood would violate their Jewish law (Lev. 17:10-14). The people did not understand the meaning of these statements, and in vs. 57 and 58, He said in effect, "All right, what I'm trying to tell you is that I live and do My miraculous works through the power of the living Father who sent Me into the world. If you will believe in Me and trust Me, you will have life. You will have a supply of food for your souls that will never run out." To "eat the bread of life" is to believe in and trust completely in Jesus and follow Him no matter what happens. It is to have the attitude that Peter had in verse 66: "To whom can I go? Christ and only Christ has the words of eternal life."

Life! [49]There was no real life[j] in that bread from the skies, which was given to your fathers in the wilderness, for they all died. [50,51]But there is such a thing as Bread from heaven giving eternal life to everyone who eats it. And I am that Living Bread that came down out of heaven. Anyone eating this Bread shall live forever; My flesh is this Bread, given to redeem humanity."

[52]Then the Jews began arguing with each other about what He meant. "How can this man give us his flesh to eat?" they asked.

[53]So Jesus said it again, "With all the earnestness I possess I tell you this: Unless you eat the flesh of the Man of Glory[k] and drink His blood, you cannot have eternal life within you. [54]But anyone who does eat My flesh and drink My blood has eternal life, and I will raise him at the Last Day. [55]For My flesh is the true food, and My blood is the true drink. [56]Everyone who eats My flesh and drinks My blood is in Me, and I in him. [57]I live by the power of the living Father who sent Me, and in the same way those who partake of Me shall live because of Me! [58]I am the true Bread from heaven; and anyone who eats this Bread shall live forever, and not die as your fathers did—though they ate bread from heaven."

How to commit political suicide

With this speech—often called the "Bread of Life" discourse, Jesus seeks to tell the people they are thinking materialistically. That is, they are thinking about things, about the political situation, about Roman oppression, about being fed.

To many in the crowd, Jesus was the walking embodiment of an unemployment check or a meal ticket so that they could ride as far as they wanted to before they decided to get off. Jesus tells the crowd that He is no meal ticket and that they don't really believe in Him or in what He is saying that He has come to do.

Because He has just fed a crowd of 5000—the incident that got the whole uproar going in the first place—Jesus refers to yesterday's miracle to try to illustrate just who He really is. He tells the people that they should eat the true Bread from heaven which is a person—Himself. If they "eat the Bread of Life" (believe in Christ and trust in Him) they'll never be hungry or thirsty again.

Jesus isn't talking about physical hunger and thirst. He is talking about inner hunger that springs from a spiritual need. In other words, Jesus knew that to fill a man's belly, to even free him from Roman oppression, is not the whole answer to helping that man live successfully.

There is a tremendous difference between "being a success" by the standards in society and "living successfully" in a genuine relationship with Christ. From the cradle, most people learn that success is measured by money, things, brains, looks, personality, etc. As life moves on (and in) they learn that none of these things are enough. One fellow learned this lesson when he came out of college and went into the army.* And he learned the important lesson from fellows who had no college degrees.

God showed Bill Colbert that he was very proud of his B.A. Like most college grads, Colbert had been careful to tell himself that he did not think "I have finally arrived" once the sheepskin was in his hand. However, as time passed he slipped into an

*See "God Used It For Good," Bill Colbert, *His*, June 1965.

79

unconscious deep-seated pride in having achieved tangible evidence of a recognizable degree of sophistication, culture and refinement.

But, God used a G.I. named Andy to stick pins in his balloon. Andy didn't do it by deliberately preaching or pointing out his own good points. He simply "ate the Bread of Life" through simple faith in Christ's promises. Andy's conscious awareness of the Holy Spirit deeply affected Bill Colbert. Because of his formal education—his "degree"—Colbert tended to seek rational explanations for everything. Through Andy, however, the Holy Spirit spoke to Colbert about his need for more love toward others.

Colbert also recalls that within three months of his conversion, Andy and one of the other fellows took on the responsibility of teaching a class of young boys about Christ and His Word. Although very young in the faith himself, Andy took this position of leadership because no one else would do it.

Andy was one of those fellows who "knows one tenth as much as we do, (but who) is doing one hundred times more for God with His blessings and our criticisms."*

You don't need a college degree, "four on the floor," or a four-point grade average to be successful. You simply need to constantly eat the Bread of Life. But in order to eat that kind of bread, you have to be hungry . . .

*A quote credited to Jim Elliot, one of the five missionaries martyred by the Auca Indians in Ecuador in 1956.

John 6:59-71

[59](He preached the above sermon in the synagogue in Capernaum.) [60]Even His disciples said, "This is very hard to understand. Who can tell what He means?"

[61]Jesus knew within Himself that His disciples were complaining and said to them, "Does *this* offend you? [62]Then what will you think if you see Me, the Son of Mankind, return to heaven again? [63]Only the Holy Spirit gives eternal life.[1] Those born only once with physical birth[m] will never receive this gift. But now I have told you how to get this true spiritual life. [64]But some of you don't believe Me."

(For Jesus knew from the beginning who didn't believe and the one who would betray Him.) [65]And He remarked, "That is what I meant when I said that no one can come to Me unless the Father attracts him to Me."

[66]At this point many of His disciples turned away and deserted Him. [67]Then Jesus turned to The Twelve and asked, "Are you going too?"

[68]Simon Peter replied, "Master, to whom shall we go? You alone have the words that give eternal life, [69]And we believe them and know You are the holy Son of God."

[70]Then Jesus said, "I chose the twelve of you, and one is a devil."

[71](He was speaking of Judas, son of Simon Iscariot, one of The Twelve, who would betray Him.)

"Lord, we came to play . . ."

Many of the so-called "followers" of Christ streamed out of the synagogue after His talk about eating the Bread of Life. They had suddenly lost their appetites. They weren't really attracted to Jesus. A person is attracted to Jesus because of an inner hunger that cannot be satisfied by barley loaves and fish, steak and French fries, or even "becoming a success."

There is nobody left now but the twelve—

Christ's closest disciples—those whom He had chosen to be with Him. He asks them if they are going to leave Him also and Simon Peter (naturally) speaks up. Not exactly known as a man with the "smarts" and not exactly looked on as a paragon of diplomacy, Peter still lays the entire matter right on the line with insight that could only come from God, "Master, to whom shall we go? You have the words of eternal life ..."

Here is the basic quality that every Christian needs if he's going to witness for Christ. Instead of choosing to seek "success" the Christian makes the choice to live successfully by knowing the living God through Christ. To put it in athletic terms, Peter told his Lord that he and the other disciples had "come to play."

Another Christian who "came to play" is Don Shinnick—all-pro linebacker with the Baltimore Colts for some ten years.

Reared in the church, Shinnick thought he was a Christian for the first 18 years of his life, but he finally discovered "I wasn't really a Christian at all. I believed in Christ like I believed in Lincoln or Washington—with my head, but not my heart."

The summer after he graduated from high school he met another football player who knew Christ in his heart as well as his head—Bob Davenport, who later became an all-American with Shinnick at UCLA and then went on to become a successful grid coach at Taylor University. At UCLA, Campus Crusade for Christ meetings helped Shinnick discover the difference between his head knowledge and a personal relationship with Christ.

Finally, Shinnick came to the place where he asked Peter's question: "To whom can I go?" He went home one night and accepted Christ and believed in Christ as his Saviour and Lord. Shinnick became a member of the 1954 UCLA squad that was rated number one in the nation and called the "Eleven from Heaven" because the entire starting team was Christian.

While with the Baltimore Colts, Shinnick has often led Bible studies and worship services for the team. A favorite speaker on college campuses during the football off-season, Shinnick comes right to the point when tough questions are asked. One of his favorite replies is "Have you really read the Bible? Have you really investigated what Jesus said and did?"

Don Shinnick is a modern day Peter who plays linebacker for the Baltimore Colts. As he says,

CHRISTIANITY IS LIKE FOOTBALL...
YOU HAVE TO GET IN THE GAME AND PLAY

"Christianity is like football. You don't really know it until you've gotten into the game and played."*

TAKE TIME . . .

Nominated but not running. Read John 6:1-15. What was the over-all effect of Jesus' miraculous feeding of 5000 people? Would you say that this situation turned into a spiritual revival or a political convention? What is the basic difference?

God or a meal ticket? Read John 6:16-26. Did Jesus think that the crowd wanted to serve Him or use Him? What about political leaders today? Do people want to serve them or use them? What is the difference?

How to do the work of God. Read John 6:27-35. What is the connection between Jesus' symbolic statement, "I am the Bread of Life," and the motives that the people had for following Him? The people thought they were hungry for bread and for political freedom. What is Jesus telling them about their real hunger?

The only way to join "Christ's party." Read John 6:36-48. People join political parties today by looking them over and deciding which will do the most for them, but Jesus tells the crowd (and us) that there is only one way to join His "party." What is that?

Final step in withdrawal from the race. Read John 6:60-65. As far as political psychology is concerned, Jesus said all the wrong things in His Bread of Life discourse. Is Jesus interested in the "political race" that people have in mind? Why not? See especially v. 63.

The only way to go. Read John 6:66-71. In vs. 68,69 Peter utters one of the great statements of all time. What choice has Peter made? Is this the basic choice that everyone must make in life? Why?

TAKE INVENTORY . . .

Think through what is more important in your life: things or persons? To put it another way, do you enjoy

*Adapted by permission from *Campus Life* Magazine. Copyright 1967, Youth for Christ International, Wheaton, Illinois.

people and use things, or do you use people and enjoy things?

Are you bored with Christianity or involved? To be "involved" doesn't mean you have to go around shouting "Hallelujah, praise the Lord!" 24 hours a day, but it does mean that Christ has a grip on your life that you can't escape and you know with Peter that you have no one else to whom you can really go.

Do you follow Christ because you are trying to use Him or serve Him? If your basic motive for being a Christian is to "get something out of it," the Bread of Life will taste stale indeed.

TAKE ACTION . . .

Talk to a Christian friend this week and share your ideas about what it means to eat the Bread of Life. Discuss with your friend this statement by William Barclay: "In the last analysis, Christianity is not a philosophy which we accept; it is not a theory to which we give our allegiance; it is not something which is thought out; it is not something which is logically arrived at. It is a personal response to Jesus Christ. It is an allegiance and love which man gives because his heart will not allow him to do anything else."

Try talking to someone you know who is supposedly a Christian but is rather turned off on the whole thing. Share ideas from John 6 with this person and see what he has to say.

CHAPTER 8

Have you reached a verdict?

Humanly speaking, Jesus' popularity continues to slide in John chapter 7. We find Him at another feast and in another fight with the Pharisees. But there are still things here to be learned about Christ and about witnessing. For instance, Jesus always brought people around to the point of a verdict. When you come face to face with the person of Christ you must make a definite choice. Accept Him completely or reject Him absolutely....

John 7:1-53

¹After this Jesus went to Galilee, going from village to village, for He wanted to stay out of Judea where the Jewish leaders were plotting His death. ²But soon it was time for the Tabernacle Ceremonies, one of the annual Jewish holidays, ³And Jesus' brothers urged Him to go to Judea for the celebration. "Go where more people can see your miracles!" they scoffed. ⁴"You can't be famous when you hide like this! If you're so great, prove it to the world!" ⁵For even His brothers didn't believe in Him. ⁶Jesus replied, "It is not the right time for Me to go now. But you can go anytime and it will make no difference, ⁷For the world can't hate you; but it does hate Me, because I accuse it of sin and evil. ⁸You go on, and I'll come later" when it is the right time." ⁹So He remained in Galilee.

¹⁰But after His brothers had left for the celebration, then He went too, though secretly, staying out of the public eye. ¹¹The Jewish leaders tried to find Him at the celebration and kept asking if anyone had seen Him. ¹²There was a lot of discussion about Him among the crowds. Some said, "He's a wonderful man," while others said, "No, he is duping the public." ¹³But no one had the courage to speak out for Him in public for fear of reprisals from the Jewish leaders.

¹⁴Then, midway through the festival, Jesus went up to the Temple and preached openly. ¹⁵The Jewish leaders were surprised when they heard Him. "How can He know so much when He's never been to our schools?" they asked.

¹⁶So Jesus told them, "I'm not teaching you My own thoughts, but those of God who sent Me. ¹⁷If any of you really determines to do God's will, then you will certainly know whether My teaching is from God or is merely My own. ¹⁸Anyone presenting his own ideas is looking for praise for himself, but anyone seeking to honor the one who sent him is a good and true person.

¹⁹None of *you* obeys the laws of Moses! So why pick on *Me* for breaking them? Why kill *Me* for this?"

²⁰The crowd replied, "You're out of your mind! Who's trying to kill you?"

²¹,²²,²³Jesus replied, "I worked on the Sabbath by healing a man, and you were surprised. But you work on the Sabbath, too, whenever you obey Moses' law of circumcision (actually, however, this tradition of circumcision is older than the Mosaic law); for if the correct time for circumcising your children falls on the Sabbath, you go ahead and do it, as you should. So why should I be condemned for making a man completely well on the Sabbath? ²⁴Think this through and you will see that I am right."

²⁵Some of the people who lived there in Jerusalem said among themselves, "Isn't this the man they are trying to kill? ²⁶But here He is preaching in public, and they say nothing to Him. Can it be that our leaders have learned, after all, that He really is the Messiah? ²⁷But how could He be? For we know where this man was born; when Christ comes, He will just appear and no one will know where He comes from."

²⁸So Jesus, in a sermon in the Temple, called out, "Yes, you know Me and where I was born and raised, but I am the representative of one you can't know, and He is Truth. ²⁹I know Him because I was with Him, and He sent Me to you."

³⁰Then the Jewish leaders sought to arrest Him; but no hand was laid on Him, for God's time had not yet come. ³¹Many among the crowds at the Temple believed on Him. "After all," they said, "what miracles do you expect the Messiah to do that this man hasn't done?"

³²When the Pharisees heard that the crowds were in this mood, they and the chief priests sent officers to arrest Jesus. ³³But Jesus told them, "[Not yet!°] I am to be here a little longer. Then I shall return to the one who sent Me. ³⁴You will search for Me but not find Me. And you won't be able to come where I am!"

³⁵The Jewish leaders were puzzled by this statement. "Where is he planning to go?" they asked. "Maybe he is thinking of leaving the country and going as a

missionary among the Jews in other lands or maybe even to the Gentiles! ³⁶What does he mean about our looking for him and not being able to find him, and, 'You won't be able to come where I am'?"

³⁷On the last day, the climax of the holidays, Jesus shouted to the crowds, "If anyone is thirsty, let him come to Me and drink. ³⁸For the Scriptures declare that rivers of living water shall flow from the inmost being of anyone who believes in Me." ³⁹(He was speaking of the Holy Spirit, who would be given to everyone believing in Him; but the Spirit had not yet been given, because Jesus had not yet returned to His glory in heaven.) ⁴⁰When the crowds heard Him say this, some of them declared, "This man surely is the prophet who will come just before the Messiah." ⁴¹,⁴²Others said, "He *is* the Messiah." Still others, "But he *can't* be! Will the Messiah come from *Galilee?* For the Scriptures clearly state that the Messiah will be born of the royal line of David, in *Bethlehem*, the village where David was born."

⁴³So the crowd was divided about Him. ⁴⁴And some wanted Him arrested, but no one touched Him.

⁴⁵The Temple police who had been sent to arrest Him returned to the chief priests and Pharisees. "Why didn't you bring him in?" they demanded.

⁴⁶"He says such wonderful things!" they mumbled. "We've never heard anything like it."

⁴⁷"So you also have been led astray?" the Pharisees mocked. ⁴⁸"Is there a single one of us Jewish rulers or Pharisees who believes he is the Messiah? ⁴⁹These stupid crowds do, yes; but what do they know about it? A curse upon them anyway!"ᵖ

⁵⁰Then Nicodemus spoke up. (Remember him? He was the Jewish leader who came secretly to interview Jesus.) ⁵¹"Is it legal to convict a man before he is even tried?" he asked.

⁵²They replied, "Are you a wretched Galilean too? Search the Scriptures and see for yourself—no prophets will come from Galilee!"

⁵³ᵠThen the meeting broke up and everybody went home.

How a gang leader reached a verdict

The Pharisees were obviously confused about Jesus. Because He was a Galilean and the Pharisees knew that no prophet could ever come out of Galilee, they rejected Him. They rejected Him without having all the facts—the obvious fact being that Jesus had been born in Bethlehem, the very town from whence the Jewish Messiah was supposed to come.

Unfortunately, people are still confused about Christ today. Many people confuse Christ and His true teachings and the true meaning of Christianity with the hyper-traditionalism of the religious establishment. This was Tom Skinner's problem. Born and reared in Harlem, Skinner was the son of a minister. In his early teens, however, he rejected Christianity because he couldn't match his concept of "Christian" with the Harlem community he knew: thousands living in rat-infested slums and two-week-old babies often found gnawed to death by rats.

Skinner wrote off the "Bible-believing-fundamental-orthodox-conservative-evangelical-Christians" because he thought that while they had Bible verses for every social problem, they didn't have what it took inside to come into Harlem and really do something about the problems there. Sadly enough, in writing off what he thought was "hyper-religious hypocrisy," Tom Skinner wrote off Jesus Christ as well, not realizing the difference between the two.

At the age of 13, Tom Skinner became a member of the Harlem Lords, one of the "up-and-coming" local teen-age gangs. He soon fought his way up to the title of undisputed leader of the gang and through his high school years lived a double life.

At school he was president of the student body, secretary of an honor society for students with averages of over 90, president of the Shakespearean society, and even president of the young people's department of his church.

In his "other life," Tom Skinner led the Harlem Lords in 15 gang fights and they never lost. But on the night before the biggest gang fight of his career —a fight that would determine his supremacy as the most powerful teen-age gang leader in all of New York—Tom Skinner heard a radio preacher's challenge to become a new creature in Christ and to give Jesus Christ a try. All of Skinner's pseudo-intellectual arguments seemed to go down the drain that night. He knew he had to reach a verdict—and he did.

On the following night—the night of the big fight —he faced his gang. Here were 129 Harlem Lords,

COULD YOU FACE 129 "HAWKS" WITH THE NEWS THAT YOU HAD BECOME A CHRISTIAN "DOVE"?

all brandishing knives and pistols. Here were 129 "hawks" and their leader was preparing to get up and tell them that he had become a "dove"—and a Christian dove at that. Skinner recalls that he was sure he wouldn't leave the room alive. Sitting directly in front of him was the number two man of the gang whose nickname was "Mop" because when he got into a gang fight he would draw blood from someone and then put his foot in it.

But Skinner did tell his gang what had happened to him—that he had committed his life to Christ and he could no longer lead the Lords. Skinner turned and walked out of the room.

Not one of the Harlem Lords moved. A couple of nights later the "Mop" cornered Skinner and said "Tom, the other night when you walked out, I was going to put my blade in your back, but I couldn't move. It was like something or somebody glued me to my seat." Before the two of them were through talking, Skinner had led the "Mop" to Christ and then the two of them went back to the gang and led five other Harlem Lords to a personal relationship with Jesus Christ.

There are many similarities between Tom Skinner's story and the events in John 7. Jesus Christ faces a hostile crowd alone and risks death in order to tell those who hate Him who He really is and what He has come to do. The final verdict of the Pharisees seemed to be completely unfavorable because no prophet could possibly come out of a slum like Galilee. Christ's words, "If any of you really determines to do God's will, then you will certainly know whether My teaching is from God or is My own," are echoed today by Tom Skinner, a Negro whose message to society is simply this:

"It doesn't make any difference if you do not accept me, because I have been accepted by the God of heaven and earth. It does not make any difference if you do not love me, maybe you cannot love me because of your built-in prejudices, your opposition to my Christian philosophy, or the color of my skin. I am already loved and accepted. All I ask is that you give me the privilege to love you. Whether or not you love me back is not important."*

Could you find a better philosophy than this for the Christian witness? Watch Jesus as He lives out that very philosophy in the next incidents recorded in John's Gospel. . .

John 8:1-59

¹Jesus returned to the Mount of Olives.
²Early the next morning He came again to the Temple. A crowd soon gathered, and He sat down and talked to them. ³As He was speaking, the Jewish leaders and Pharisees brought a woman caught in adultery and placed her out in front of the staring crowd. ⁴"Teacher," they said to Jesus, "This woman was caught in the very act of adultery. ⁵Moses' law says to kill her. What about it?"
⁶They were trying to trap Him into saying something they could use against Him. But Jesus stooped down and wrote in the dust with His finger. ⁷They kept demanding an answer, so He stood up again and said, "All right, hurl the stones at her until she

*Adapted from "What's the Next Move?" by Tom Skinner, *Collegiate Challenge*, Spring 1968, p. 14.

dies. But only he who never sinned may throw the first!" ⁸Then He stooped down again and wrote some more in the dust. ⁹And the Jewish leaders slipped away one by one, beginning with the eldest, until only Jesus was left in front of the crowd with the woman.

¹⁰Then Jesus stood up again and said to her, "Where are your accusers? Didn't even one of them condemn you?"

¹¹"No, sir," she said.

And Jesus said, "Neither do I. Go and sin no more."

¹²Later, in one of His talks, Jesus said to the people, "I am the Light of the world. So if you follow Me, you won't be stumbling through the darkness, for living light will flood your path."

¹³The Pharisees replied, "You are boasting—and lying!"

¹⁴Jesus told them, "These claims are true even though I make them concerning Myself. For I know where I came from and where I am going, but you don't know this about Me. ¹⁵You pass judgment on Me without knowing the facts. I am not judging you now; ¹⁶But if I were, it would be an absolutely correct judgment in every respect, for I have with Me the Father who sent Me. ¹⁷Your laws say that if two men agree on something that has happened, their witness is accepted as fact. ¹⁸Well, I am one witness and My Father who sent Me is the other."

¹⁹"Where is your father?" they asked.

Jesus answered, "You don't know who I am, so you don't know who My Father is. If you knew Me, then you would know Him too."

²⁰Jesus made these statements while in the section of the Temple known as the Treasury. But He was not arrested, for His time had not yet run out.

²¹Later He said to them again, "I am going away; and you will search for Me, and die in your sins. And you cannot come where I am going."

²²The Jews asked, "Is he planning suicide? What does he mean, 'You cannot come where I am going'?"

²³Then He said to them, "You are from below; I am from above. You are of this world; I am not. ²⁴That is why I said that you will die in your sins; for unless you believe that I am the Messiah, the Son of God, you will die in your sins."

²⁵"Tell us who you are," they demanded.

He replied, "I am the one I have always claimed to be. ²⁶I could condemn you for much and teach you much, but I won't, for I say only what I am told to by the one who sent Me; and He is Truth."

²⁷But they still didn't understand that He was talking to them about God. ²⁸So Jesus said, "When you have killed the Man of Glory, then you will realize that I am He and that I have not been telling you My own ideas, but have spoken what the Father taught Me. ²⁹And He who sent Me is with Me—He has not deserted Me—for I always do those things that are pleasing to Him." ³⁰Then many of the Jewish leaders who heard Him say these things began believing Him to be the Messiah.

³¹Jesus said to them, "You are truly My disciples if you live as I tell you to, ³²And you will know the truth, and the truth will set you free."

³³"But we are descendants of Abraham," they said, "and have never been slaves to any man on earth! What do You mean, 'set free'?"

³⁴Jesus replied, "You are slaves to sin, every one of you. ³⁵And slaves don't have rights, but the Son has every right there is! ³⁶So if the Son sets you free, you will indeed be free—³⁷(Yes, I realize that you are descendants of Abraham!) And yet some of you are trying to kill Me because My message does not find a home within your hearts. ³⁸I am telling you what I saw when I was with My Father. But you are following the advice of *your* father."

³⁹"Our father is Abraham," they declared.

"No!" Jesus replied, "for if he were, you would follow his good example. ⁴⁰But instead you are trying to kill Me—and all because I told you the truth I heard from God. Abraham wouldn't do a thing like that! ⁴¹No, you are obeying your *real* father when you act that way."

They replied, "We were not born out of wedlock— our true Father is God Himself."

⁴²Jesus told them, "If that were so, then you would love Me, for I have come to you from God. I am not here on My own, but He sent Me. ⁴³Why can't you understand what I am saying? It is because you are prevented from doing so! ⁴⁴For you are children of your father the Devil and you love to do the evil things he does. He was a murderer from the beginning and a hater of truth—there is not an iota of truth in him. When he lies, it is perfectly normal; for he is the father of liars. ⁴⁵And so when I tell the truth, you just naturally don't believe it! ⁴⁶Which of you can truthfully accuse Me of one single sin? [No one!ᵗ] And since I am telling you the truth, why don't you believe Me? ⁴⁷Anyone whose Father is God listens gladly to the words of God. Since you don't, it proves you aren't His children."

⁴⁸"You Samaritan! Foreigner! Devil" the Jewish leaders snarled. "Didn't we say all along you were possessed by a demon?"

⁴⁹"No," Jesus said, "I have no demon in Me. For I honor My Father—and you dishonor Me. ⁵⁰And though I have no wish to make Myself great, God wants this for Me and judges [those who reject Meᵘ]. ⁵¹With all the earnestness I have I tell you this—no one who obeys Me shall ever die!"

⁵²The leaders of the Jews said, "Now we know you are possessed by a demon. Even Abraham and the mightiest prophets died, and yet you say that obeying you will keep a man from dying! ⁵³So you are greater than our father Abraham, who died? And greater than the prophets, who died? Who do you think you are?"

⁵⁴Then Jesus told them this: "If I am merely boasting about Myself, it doesn't count. But it is My Father— and you claim Him as your God—who is saying these

glorious things about Me. ⁵⁵But you do not even know Him. I do. If I said otherwise, I would be as great a liar as you! But it is true—I know Him and fully obey Him. ⁵⁶Your father Abraham rejoiced to see My day. He knew I was coming and was glad."

⁵⁷*The Jewish leaders:* "You aren't even 50 years old—sure, you've seen Abraham!"

⁵⁸*Jesus:* "The absolute truth is that I was in existence before Abraham was ever born!"

⁵⁹At that point the Jewish leaders picked up stones to kill Him. But Jesus was hidden from them, and walked past them and left the Temple.

What do you think of Jesus?

As Jesus' debate with the Pharisees continues, the issues that divide Him and His mission from them and their pat religious system become increasingly sharp. These very same issues divide Christians from a world that meets Christ but refuses to accept Him for who He is—precisely the mortal mistake of the Pharisees.

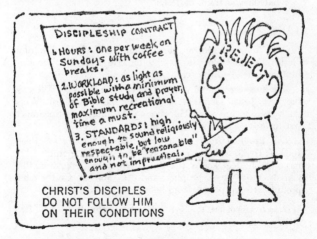

DISCIPLESHIP CONTRACT

1. HOURS: one per week on Sundays with coffee breaks.

2. WORKLOAD: as light as possible with a minimum of Bible study and prayer; maximum recreational time a must.

3. STANDARDS: high enough to sound religiously respectable, but low enough to be "reasonable" and not impractical.

REJECT

CHRIST'S DISCIPLES DO NOT FOLLOW HIM ON THEIR CONDITIONS

Dr. Richard Halverson sums up chapter 8 of John precisely. He writes ...

Reduced to simplest terms, this is the issue: Either a man goes *all the way* with Jesus Christ—or he should reject Him as a fraud or a fool.

There is *no rational half-way measure* with Jesus Christ.

Some men try to treat Him as a great teacher—and *then choose which of His teachings they will accept* ...

Thus becoming His judge.

Others think of Jesus as the finest example of what men ought to be ...

Yet *refuse to follow His example*—or take seriously what He said.

Their attitude is beneath contempt.

If a man will not accept what Jesus said concerning Himself, then he should, in honesty, repudiate Jesus as a deceiver or an egomaniac.

To attempt to honor Him *while rejecting His claims* is dishonest and irrational.

Jesus Himself refused disciples *who came on their own conditions.*

With Him it was all or nothing ...

Either He is Lord ... or unworthy of consideration.

What do *you* think of Jesus?*

TAKE TIME ...

The "fugitive" returns. Read John 7:1-13. Why did Jesus "hide out" in Galilee and why did He send His sneering brothers ahead to the feast in Jerusalem?

The sure-fire test of Jesus' claims. John 7:14-36. What is the test Jesus claims that He Himself describes? What does Jesus mean when He says not to judge by appearance but to judge with right judgment?

The prophet from the wrong side of the tracks. Read John 7:37-53. Who re-enters the story at this point? What basic prejudice keeps the Pharisees from believing that Christ could be a prophet and the Son of God? What prejudices keep people from believing in Christ today?

*Perspective, Volume 19, No. 8, March 1, 1967, Richard C. Halverson.

Let fly with the stones, if . . . Read John 8:1-11. Do you agree with Jesus' decision in this case? Isn't Jesus condoning adultery by not declaring that the woman should be stoned? What does this story teach you about the difference in condemning someone and recognizing their needs?

Why won't men see the Light? Read John 8:12-20. Why do people turn from the Light of the World and make their own way through the darkness? Is it possible for light to be too bright? In what way? Does Christ's light sometimes become too bright for your life? How?

Is He planning suicide? Read John 8:21-30. Especially vs. 24,25. What did Jesus mean when He said "You cannot come where I am going"? What kept many of the Jews from believing in Christ? What keeps people from believing in Christ today?

The truth will set you free. Read John 8:31-59. According to this passage, what is the difference between freedom and slavery? Could a person be in chains and still be free? In what way?

TAKE INVENTORY . . .

What do you really think of Jesus? Take a lot of time with your answer. How many reasons can you give for what you think of Jesus Christ?

TAKE ACTION . . .

Write a letter to someone this week and explain to this person how you have been set free because you know the truth.

Do some simple act that shows Christ is your Lord as well as your Saviour and that you want to follow His example. For instance, do you have a habit you haven't submitted to Him? Perhaps you have a hard time finding your temper because you are always losing it. Or perhaps you could do an act of kindness for someone—especially someone who you don't particularly like. Or perhaps you could pay a sincere compliment to that person who essentially makes you green with envy or crimson with disgust. There are many "small ways" to follow Christ daily. Try some of them and see what happens.

99

Before I met Christ, I used to think no guy could be more mixed up than I was. Now I've found — forgiveness, as well as strength and direction that really amaze me!

The unanswerable argument

It was a senseless murder. Two teen-agers had shot a local store owner seven times ("execution style") in a hold-up that had netted them all of $70, a bottle of vodka, and some cigarettes.

How could you possibly talk to someone like this and share Christ with him? That was the challenge that faced Jack Dee of San Jose, Calif. Jack knew one of the two murderers very well. In fact he had gone to school with Raul Vasquez. When he heard about what Raul had done, he felt he had to try to get through to him.

What happened? Let Raul tell you in his own words:

"Something has happened to me since that terrible crime. When I was out in the streets I never believed in God. But a young man has been to see me, and he told me how I could open the door of my life to the Lord and let him come in. I did that and now I am changed. Every night before I go to sleep I pray to God that he will help the man's family to survive through the years to come. I hope they won't hate me forever for what I have done. I know that I can't change what has happened, but I am praying I can make something good out of my future."*

Had Raul really changed? Only time can tell, and as he wrote those words in a letter back to Jack Dee he faced a great deal of time in prison for his crime. A teen-ager who tried to gain an enlarged perspective of life with drugs like LSD, Raul Vasquez was actually blinded by the drugs and other substitutes for the life that he tried to obtain. It took a man's death by his hand, and trial, and prison, to help Raul see, but above all, it took a Christian friend who was concerned enough to share Christ.

There is a story in John 9. It's a story about a blind man who became able to see, and seeing people who remained as blind as Raul Vasquez was when he shot that store owner. Blindness, you see, is not necessarily a disease of the optic nerve or retina. Blindness, the kind of blindness that can be cured by that Light of the world, goes much deeper than that...

John 9:1-41

[1]As He was walking along, He saw a man blind from birth.

*From the article, "Tell It Like It Is," by Gordon McLean, *Campus Life*, p. 38.

²"Master," His disciples asked Him, "why was this man born blind? Was it a result of his own sins or those of his parents?"

³"Neither," Jesus answered. "But to demonstrate the power of God. ⁴All of us must quickly carry out the tasks assigned us by the one who sent Me, for there is little time left before the night falls and all work comes to an end. ⁵But while I am still here in the world, I give it My light."

⁶Then He spat on the ground and made mud from the spittle and smoothed the mud over the blind man's eyes, ⁷And told him, "Go and wash in the Pool of Siloam" (the word "Siloam" means "Sent"). So the man went where he was sent and washed and came back seeing!

⁸His neighbors and others who knew him as a blind beggar asked each other, "Is this the same fellow—that beggar?"

⁹Some said yes, and some said no. "It can't be the same man," they thought, "but he surely looks like him!"

And the beggar said, "I *am* the same man!"

¹⁰Then they asked him how in the world he could see. What had happened?

¹¹And he told them, "A man they call Jesus made mud and smoothed it over my eyes and told me to go to the Pool of Siloam and wash off the mud. I did, and I can see!"

¹²"Where is he now?" they asked.

"I don't know," he replied.

¹³Then they took the man to the Pharisees. ¹⁴Now as it happened, this all occurred on a Sabbath.ᵛ ¹⁵Then the Pharisees asked him all about it. So he told them how Jesus had smoothed the mud over his eyes, and when it was washed away, he could see!

¹⁶Some of them said, "Then this fellow Jesus is not from God, because he is working on the Sabbath!"

Others said, "But how could an ordinary sinner do such miracles?" So there was deep division of opinion among them. ¹⁷Then the Pharisees turned on the man who had been blind and demanded, "This man who opened your eyes—who do you say he is?"

"I think He must be a prophet sent from God," the man replied.

[18]The Jewish leaders wouldn't believe he had been blind, until they called in his parents [19]And asked them, "Is this your son? Was he born blind? If so, how can he see?"

[20]His parents replied, "We know this is our son and that he was born blind, [21]But we don't know what happened to make him see, or who did it. He is old enough to speak for himself. Ask him!"

[22,23]They said this in fear of the Jewish leaders who had announced that anyone saying Jesus was the Messiah would be excommunicated.

[24]So for the second time they called in the man who had been blind and told him, "Give the glory to God, not to Jesus, for we know Jesus is an evil person."

[25]"I don't know whether He is good or bad," the man replied, "but I know this: *I was blind, and now I see!*"

[26]"But what did he do?" they asked. "How did he heal you?"

[27]"Look!" the man exclaimed, "I told you once; didn't you listen? Why do you want to hear it again? Do you want to become His disciples too?"

[28]Then they cursed him and said, "You are his disciple, but we are disciples of Moses.

[29]"We know God has spoken to Moses, but as for this fellow, we don't know anything about him."

[30]"Why, that's very strange!" the man replied. "He can heal blind men, but you don't know anything about Him! [31]Well, God doesn't listen to evil men, but He has open ears to those who worship Him and do His will. [32]Since the world began there has never been anyone who could open the eyes of someone born blind. [33]If this man were not from God, He couldn't do it."

[34]"You illegitimate bastard," you!" they shouted. "Are you trying to teach *us?*" And they threw him out.

[35]When Jesus heard what had happened, He found the man and said, "Do you believe in the Messiah?"[x]

[36]The man answered, "Who is He, sir, for I want to."

[37]"You have seen Him," Jesus said, "and He is speaking to you!"

[38]"Yes, Lord," the man said, "I believe!" And he worshiped Jesus.

[39]Then Jesus told him, "I have come into the world to give sight to those who are spiritually blind and to show those who think they see that they are blind."

[40]The Pharisees who were standing there asked, "Are you saying we are blind?"

[41]"If you were blind, you wouldn't be guilty," Jesus replied. "But your guilt remains because you claim to know what you are doing."

A murderer hears the unanswerable argument

There are many appealing things about this story. It just isn't an incident where a blind man regains his sight. This is a story of how a man becomes rightly related to his God and "sees" completely for the first time in his life. While this beggar, who had been blind from birth, couldn't explain everything that had happened to him in minute detail to the badgering Pharisees, one thing he did know: that once he had been blind but now, because he had met Christ, he could see.

As for the Pharisees, Jesus plainly told them that while they had 20-20 vision when it came to any slight infractions of their precious laws, they were as spiritually blind as the proverbial bat. The reason for their blindness was the fact that they could not see—their sin. As long as a person can't see his sin or his need for God's forgiveness and salvation, he will remain blind.

THOSE WHO CAN'T SEE THEIR SIN REMAIN BLIND.

Jack Dee, the teen-ager who became concerned for murderer Raul Vasquez, knew perfectly well that Raul was blind. Jack knew Raul was blind because he had suffered from this same kind of blindness himself. In an effort to help Raul see the light, Jack wrote him a letter that had the same unanswerable argument voiced by the blind man in the ninth chapter of John. Part of that letter follows...

"It's funny, Raul, how two guys will see each other every day at school, think they know each other, but never talk about the most important things. There's something really important I should have told you—you'll never know how sorry I am that I didn't. Just about mid-term something happened in my life that really made it different and changed my whole outlook on everything. I realized that there was something more important than living for my own selfish interests ... that God has a wonderful plan for my life, and that through Jesus Christ I can find it. That's when I received Him into my life.

"Believe me, Raul, I'm not trying to play the preacher role. I've got a long road ahead of me in my own life, but I'm glad that at least I've started on the right track. Maybe things look kind of dark and discouraging for you, but my experience has shown me that God loves every one of us. You know, before I met Christ I used to think that no guy could be more mixed up than I was. Now I've found forgiveness, as well as strength and direction, that really amazes me."*

Jack Dee's words can hardly be called a short course in theology. He doesn't even quote any Bible verses. What he does quote, and more important, what he does communicate, is that once he had been blind in his entire outlook on life, and then Christ made him see.

There is no substitute for personal experience with Jesus Christ. There is no argument against a witness that can share a personal experience with Jesus Christ.

TAKE TIME ...

Do you suffer because you sin? Read John 9:1-7. Compare Deut. 5:9 and Num. 14:18 to get ideas on Old Testament passages that seem to teach a relationship between sin and suffering. Jesus' answer to His disciples'

*From the article, "Tell It Like It Is," Gordon McLean, *Campus Life*, p. 38.

question (vs. 3,4) is actually a partial answer to one of life's basic questions: "Why is there suffering in the world?"

Why bother with spit and clay? Read John 9:6-12. Why does Jesus go through this involved (and somewhat repulsive) routine when He could have healed the blind man with a wave of His hand? Was He trying to make things difficult or was He trying to develop a certain response in the beggar? What response?

How can a man of God break "the Law"? Read John 9:13-16. Why are the Pharisees divided in their opinion of Jesus' healing the blind man on the Sabbath? What do these verses tell you about the difference between preconceived religious prejudices and walking in faith that is essentially interested in having God work?

Why is secondhand knowledge uncertain? Read John 9:17-23. Compare replies to the Pharisees made by the blind man and his parents. Who was more certain in his conviction? What is keeping the parents from making a decisive statement? What keeps many Christians today from being more decisive in their opinions about Jesus Christ?

A thinking man's religion? Read John 9:24-34. Analyze how the blind man begins to start thinking for himself. What does he say in v. 25 that gets him started? Is the man's reasoning solid? Why won't the Pharisees listen to him?

Do you believe in him? Read John 9:35-38. Would the blind man's healing have meant a great deal if he had not come to where he could "see" who Jesus really was? Is the "unanswerable argument" also the inescapable necessity? Why?

Have you become "blind" in order to "see"? Read John 9:39-41. What is Jesus trying to tell the Pharisees? Can the "Light of the world" help anyone who thinks he can see perfectly by himself? Why not?

TAKE INVENTORY . . .

Analyze why certain people you know are effective witnesses for Christ? Is it because they are brilliant theologians and masterful Bible scholars, or is it because of one unanswerable argument—their lives show that they have experienced Jesus Christ?

Analyze your own attempts to witness. What do you find? Keep in mind that you might not find perfection, but what you are looking for is the conviction that you have experienced Christ and that you have moved from blindness to His kind of light. People aren't looking for perfection (in fact, perfection scares them away), but they are looking for real people who have had a real experience and who know a real Christ.

TAKE ACTION . . .

Sit down and write out a statement that begins "I know I have experienced a change in my life through Jesus Christ because . . ." After finishing your statement, share it with someone else—a non-Christian, if possible.

CHAPTER 10

Do you have to get involved?

New York...April, 1964...not long after midnight, and the screams of pretty young Kitty Genovese pierce the night. As she tries to reach the safety of her apartment house, a killer stabs her again and again, taking a half an hour to kill her.

All this time Kitty is screaming, pleading for help: "Oh my God! He stabbed me! Please help me. I'm dying! I'm dying!"

Does anyone hear her? Oh yes, 38 people in all, but no one makes any move to help her. No one even calls the police! Later, these 38 "witnesses" tell investigating officers that they just didn't want to get involved...

Los Angeles, February, 1965. A girl gets into her car after work and is attacked by a man with a beer can opener. With the beer can opener at her throat, she is forced to drive through California rush hour traffic. At stop lights, the girl screams, drivers look her way, see the crazed maniac beside her slashing her throat and chest with the beer can opener, and then she is forced to drive on. No one makes a move to help. Finally, she succeeds in jumping from the car. She dashes to a nearby porch where a woman is standing. The woman jumps inside the door and slams it in the girl's face. About this time the girl is thinking that she is "pretty disgusted with the whole human race." She finally manages to save herself by running a mile to a friend's house and safety.

Incidents of people being attacked and left unaided by others who "don't want to get involved" are not uncommon.

What keeps people from "getting involved" when an innocent person's life is in danger? Is it merely fear? Or does it go deeper than that? Is there any connection between this type of "non-involvement" and the indifference that many Christians show to people who don't know Christ as Saviour? Isn't life at stake here as well? What did Jesus have to say about this question of involvement? Did He "get involved"? Let's pick up a story from the last chapter where He has healed a blind man and become quite involved in a vital argument with the Pharisees who want to kill Him for breaking their Sabbath laws. As John 10 opens, the argument is still going on . . .

¹"Anyone refusing to walk through the gate into a sheepfold, who sneaks over the wall, must surely be a thief! ²For a shepherd comes through the gate! ³The gatekeeper opens the gate for him, and the sheep hear his voice and come to him; and he calls his own sheep by name and leads them out. ⁴He walks ahead of them; and they follow him, for they recognize his voice. ⁵They won't follow a stranger, but will run from him, for they don't recognize his voice."

⁶Those who heard Jesus use this illustration didn't understand what He meant, ⁷So He explained it to them. "I am the Gate for the sheep," He said. ⁸"All others who came before Me were thieves and robbers. But the true sheep did not listen to them. ⁹Yes, I am the Gate. Those who come in by way of the Gate will be saved and will go in and out and find green pastures. ¹⁰The thief's purpose is to steal, kill and destroy. My purpose is to give eternal life—abundantly! ¹¹I am the Good Shepherd. The Good Shepherd lays down His life for the sheep. ¹²A hired man will run when he sees a wolf coming and will leave the sheep, for they aren't his and he isn't their shepherd. And so the wolf leaps on them and scatters the flock. ¹³The hired man runs because he is hired and has no real concern for the sheep. ¹⁴I am the Good Shepherd and know My own sheep, and they know Me, ¹⁵Just as My Father knows Me and I know the Father; and I lay down My life for the sheep.

¹⁶"I have other sheep, too, in another fold. I must bring them also, and they will heed My voice; and there will be one flock with one Shepherd. ¹⁷The Father loves Me because I lay down My life that I may have it back again. ¹⁸No one can kill Me without My consent—I lay down My life voluntarily. For I have the right and power to lay it down when I want to and also the right and power to take it again. For the Father has given Me this right."

¹⁹When He said these things, the Jewish leaders

111

were again divided in their opinions about Him. ²⁰Some of them said, "He has a demon or else is crazy. Why listen to a man like that?"

²¹Others said, "This doesn't sound to us like a man possessed by a demon! Can a demon open the eyes of blind men?"

²²,²³It was winter,ʸ and Jesus was in Jerusalem at the time of the Dedication Celebration. He was at the Temple, walking through the section known as Solomon's Hall. ²⁴The Jewish leaders surrounded Him and asked, "How long are you going to keep us in suspense? If you are the Messiah, tell us plainly."

²⁵"I have already told you,ᶻ and you didn't believe Me," Jesus replied. "The proof is in the miracles I do in the name of My Father. ²⁶But you don't believe Me because you are not part of My flock. ²⁷My sheep recognize My voice, and I know them, and they follow Me. ²⁸I give them eternal life, and they shall never perish. No one shall snatch them away from Me, ²⁹For My Father has given them to Me, and He is more powerful than anyone else, so no one can kidnap them from Me. ³⁰I and the Father are one."

³¹Then again the Jewish leaders picked up stones to kill Him. ³²Jesus said, "At God's direction I have done many a miracle to help the people. For which one are you killing Me?"

³³They replied, "Not for any good work, but for blasphemy; you, a mere man, have declared yourself to be God."

³⁴,³⁵,³⁶"In your own Law it says that men are gods!" He replied. "So if the Scripture, which cannot be untrue, speaks of those as gods to whom the message of God came, do you call it blasphemy when the one sanctified and sent into the world by the Father says, 'I am the Son of God'? ³⁷Don't believe Me unless I do miracles of God. ³⁸But if I do, believe them even if you don't believe Me! Then you will become convinced that the Father is in Me, and I in the Father."

³⁹Once again they started to arrest Him. But He

A living example of "over my dead body"

A Palestinian shepherd vowed that wolves, bears or robbers would enter his sheepfold "over his dead body" and he literally meant exactly that. Hillside sheepfolds in Palestine were just spaces enclosed by a wall of stones. The shepherd guarded his flocks by sitting down or lying across the entrance, so that nothing could get past without his knowledge. In a literal sense, the shepherd was the door or gate of the sheepfold. Jesus used this illustration to picture Himself as the door to salvation or safety, because it is through Him all men have access to God (see Eph. 2:18, Heb. 10:20).

walked away and left them, ⁴⁰And went beyond the Jordan River to stay near the place where John was first baptizing. ⁴¹And many followed Him. "John didn't do miracles," they remarked to one another, "but all his predictions concerning this man have come true."

⁴²And many came to the decision that He was the Messiah.ᵃ

He "got involved" in Viet Nam

One thing about a Palestinian shepherd. He was no pansy. He definitely had to "get involved" if he wanted to keep his sheep and himself alive. Lions, bears, thieves and robbers were all real dangers to him and his sheep.

Jesus used this allegory about sheep and shepherds to tell the Pharisees they were false leaders of the people, but there is something being said

IT'S ONE THING TO MAKE RELIGIOUS NOISES,
IT'S ANOTHER TO GET INTO THE BATTLE

here for today's Christian as well. When Jesus calls Himself the "good shepherd," He is telling all Christians to get involved with other people just as He did. It's one thing to spout theories and make religious noises on Sunday morning; it's another to get into the thick of the battle—to get with people and let them know you care.

Take, for example, Chaplain Bernie Windmiller who served in the Viet Nam war. Windmiller didn't deal out sermons and gospel tracts from the safety of a chapel back at base camp. He believed in going right into the battle with his men—into the mud and jungle, into nights where he would have to sleep soaking wet in underbrush so thick he couldn't find a place to lie down.

Once a sergeant told Windmiller, "Chaplain, you are a real infantryman's chaplain—the best I've seen in a long time."

Of course, this was flattering to hear, but Windmiller didn't risk his life simply to collect compliments. Some of his men would ask him if he had to come into the field with them and risk his life. When Windmiller told them that no, he didn't have to come, the men replied by saying they thought he was crazy. Then Windmiller would tell them why he chose to come—to be with them and minister to them when they needed him the most.

"I really feel this," he wrote home in one letter. "I must be where my men are to do them any good—for someday I may be able to snatch some from the burning."

Plenty of times for "burning" came to Windmiller and his outfit. Here are just a few samples of the kind of action he described in letters he wrote back to his family in the states:

"The V.C. burst of fire wounded three men in our Charlie blitzer element. So I dropped my pack and started up among the rice paddy to reach those wounded men. I was scared, but I kept my head. I knew I had to help those men . . ."

"Duffy (a soldier who joined Windmiller's company) is a real honest guy and I like him. I hope I'm able to stay close to him—I feel the Holy Spirit will draw him to Christ yet. Really feel that he will be a life-long friend. These are good relationships and I thank God for them. These you would never get in a parish situation. People are too involved in clichés and systems. It's great being a servant of Christ out in the raw of life . . ."

"I bummed a ride over to the 93rd evac where I had 16 men. Some I knew well—others were just acquaintances.

115

But they were my men and it hurts to see each one. One of my dear Negro sergeant friends, a fine Christian, had his left arm blown off at the shoulder and sustained head and face wounds. He looked terrible and could barely talk. As soon as I saw him, he said, 'I was talking to the Lord all the time, and He heard me.' I prayed with him before I left and could not hold back the tears."

"This kind of battle will come again, but this is what our faith in Christ is for. We must trust Him. I do what has to be done and nothing foolish. I did a lot of praying yesterday and last night, but that is why we have God, to let us live a day at a time . . ."*

Living a day at a time and being involved. Perhaps you will never lie in the mud in a raging battle with death dropping all around you (and then again, perhaps you will). But you don't need battles and mud and death around you to get involved. Chaplain Windmiller didn't really have to get involved and go out in the battle field, but he did anyway because he had a drive inside of him that could let him do nothing else. In his own way and his own time in history, this chaplain became a good shepherd—willing to lay down his life for the sheep.

TAKE TIME . . .

Use the following ideas to take time for a second look at John chapter 10 and apply it to your life and the daily situations that only you face.

The Good Shepherd allegory. Read John 10:1-6. Jesus is still arguing with the Pharisees, who He has just called blind because they think they can see. Now He talks to them in the form of an allegory and mentions the sheep fold, the good shepherd, thieves and robbers. Who is the

*Material on Chaplain Bernie Windmiller adapted from the article "God, Spare Him!", *Campus Life*, October 1967.

"shepherd"? Who are the strangers that the sheep will not follow?

Hired hands don't get involved. Read John 10:7-13. What is the difference between a true shepherd and a hireling who is in it just for the money? Why is a person happier in his work if he can be in it for more than "just the money"? Why is a Christian happier if he can witness because there is more in it than just "his duty"?

One flock, one shepherd. Read John 10:14-16. Compare with Isa. 56:8 and Eph. 2:14. Is there an answer here for civil rights strife, racial prejudice and bigotry? What is that answer?

The greatest power of all. Read John 10:17,18. Could these words be spoken by anyone beside God Himself? Why?

He has a demon, is crazy, or . . . Read John 10:19-21. The Pharisees were arguing here about the key issue concerning Jesus Christ. What is that key issue? Is it still the key issue today? How do you feel about Jesus Christ?

Lunatic or Lord of all life? Read the entire passage, John 10:1-21. Speeches like this from a mere man would sound like the raving of a lunatic. What is there about Jesus that convinces you that He was no lunatic?

TAKE INVENTORY . . .

Think through the basic question that comes out of this chapter from John: "Am I really willing to get personally involved with others?" And then a second question: "Do I sometimes get personally involved with others out of real concern for them, or do I do it as a duty in order to communicate Christ?"

TAKE ACTION . . .

Think about your friends, acquaintances, members of your family. Is there anyone to whom you could show more personal interest? (Romantic interests should not be included here.) Why not make a move right now to get to know this person better, to do something with him or her that shows personal interest on your part?

Is there any project, group or cause in which you can become personally involved? How involved, for example, are you in your activities at church? How involved are you in community affairs and groups at school?

117

CHAPTER 11

Can you really be sure?

"Can a person be sure he'll go to heaven?"

This was the question put to 18 people in Chicago's Union Station by WMBI radio announcer Walter Carson. Here are some of the answers he got . . .

"Of course not."

"Why not?"

"Well, first you have to know whether there is a heaven."

"What is your feeling on that?"

"I don't believe so. It just seems a bit improbable to me. I think once you're dead, that's it."

That was the opinion of a student from nearby Northwestern University. A Chicago lawyer answered the question this way.

"I think so."

"How can you be sure?"

"By living a good life."

"What is involved in living a good life?"

"Well, I believe living by the Ten Commandments would probably be the best way to explain it."

A traveler from Philadelphia answered like this:

"No, I don't think nobody can be sure of that, but they can sure try to make sure they will."

"What's involved in trying to?"

"Well, living a good life."

"What do you think is involved in living the right kind of life."

"Don't murder people or be two-faced or anything like that. Live an honest life."

A salesman replied by saying a person would be sure to go to heaven "if he obeyed the rules of his religion." He did not volunteer to explain what happens when the rules of one religion differ from another—or even contradict.

A railroader from West Virginia said that, "Believing is mostly involved."

"Believing in what, sir?"

"Believing that there is something at the end of life. If you don't believe, well—there's nothing to go for."

A Chicago bookkeeper answered by saying that she believed in reincarnation.

A serviceman from Missouri en route to Viet Nam said, "I don't think about it much." He admitted that he went to church but also commented, "That don't say I'm a Christian."

Out of 18 people interviewed in Chicago's Union Station on the question, "Can a person be sure he'll go to heaven?" not one of the 18 was sure that he would go or that anyone could be sure. Not one of the 18 mentioned the name of Jesus Christ.

At least four people thought it was presumptuous for anyone to say he was sure of going to heaven. A housewife from Wisconsin: "It's out of our hands completely. We all believe in God but it's a matter of our life here on earth, and I don't think any of us can say we're good and will go to heaven."

A student from Germany: "I think if I were God I would know. I don't think anybody could know... I think it's a privilege of God which God can grant us, but I don't think we can be sure."

A college student from Ohio: "I don't think you can really be sure of anything."

Out of the entire 18 no one was sure that he would go to heaven or that anyone could be sure.

And not one of the 18 mentioned the name of Jesus Christ.[*]

Is there a way to be sure that you're sure? Read John's account of the raising of Lazarus from the dead and decide for yourself. . . .

John 11:1-57

[1,2]Do you remember Mary, who poured the costly perfume on Jesus' feet and wiped them with her hair?[b] Well, her brother Lazarus, who lived in Bethany with Mary and her sister Martha, was sick. [3]So the two sisters sent a message to Jesus telling Him, "Sir, your good friend is very, very sick."

[4]But when Jesus heard about it, He said, "The purpose of his illness is not death, but for the glory of God. I, the Son of God, will receive glory from this situation."

[5]Although Jesus was very fond of Martha, Mary and Lazarus, [6]He stayed where He was for the next two days and made no move to go to them. [7]Finally, after the two days, He said to His disciples, "Let's go to Judea."

[8]But His disciples objected. "Master," they said, "only a few days ago the Jewish leaders in Judea were trying to kill You. Are You going there again?"

[9]Jesus replied, "There are 12 hours of daylight every day, and during every hour of it a man can walk safely and not stumble. [10]Only at night is there danger of a wrong step because of the dark."

[11]Then He said, "Our friend Lazarus has gone to sleep, but now I will go and waken him!"

[12,13]The disciples, thinking Jesus meant Lazarus was having a good night's rest, said, "That means he is getting better!" But Jesus meant Lazarus had died.

[14]Then He told them plainly, "Lazarus is dead. [15]And for your sake, I am glad I wasn't there, for this will

*Taken from "No One Was Sure . . ." *Moody Monthly,* January 1967, p. 32.

give you another opportunity to believe in Me. Come, let's go to him."

¹⁶Thomas, nicknamed "The Twin," said to his fellow disciples, "Let's go too—and die with Him."

¹⁷When they arrived at Bethany, they were told that Lazarus had already been in his tomb for four days! ¹⁸Bethany was only a couple of miles down the road from Jerusalem, ¹⁹And many of the Jewish leaders had come to pay their respects and to console Martha and Mary on their loss. ²⁰When Martha got word that Jesus was coming, she went to meet Him. But Mary stayed at home.

²¹Martha said to Jesus, "Sir, if You had been here, my brother wouldn't have died. ²²And even now it's not too late, for I know that God will bring my brother back to life again, if You will only ask Him to."

²³Jesus told her, "Your brother will come back to life again."

²⁴"Yes," Martha said, "when everyone else does, on Resurrection Day."

²⁵Jesus told her, "I am the one who raises the dead and gives them life again. Anyone who believes in Me, even though he dies like anyone else, shall live again. ²⁶He is given eternal life for believing in Me and shall never perish.ᶜ Do you believe this, Martha?"

²⁷"Yes, Master," she told Him. "I believe You are the Messiah, the Son of God, the one we have so long awaited." ²⁸Then she left Him and returned to Mary and calling her aside from the mourners told her, "He is here and wants to see you."

²⁹Mary left immediately to go to Him. ³⁰Now Jesus had stayed outside the village, at the place where Martha met Him. ³¹When the Jewish leaders who were at the house trying to console Mary saw her hastily leave, they assumed she was going to Lazarus' tomb to weep; so they followed her.

³²When Mary arrived where Jesus was, she fell down at His feet, saying, "Sir, if You had been here, my brother would still be alive."

³³When Jesus saw her weeping and the Jewish leaders wailing with her, He was moved with indignation and deeply troubled.

³⁴"Where is he buried?" He asked them.

They told Him, "Come and see."

³⁵Tears came to Jesus' eyes.

³⁶"They were close friends," the Jewish leaders said. "See how much he loved him." ³⁷But some said, "This fellow healed a blind man—why couldn't he keep Lazarus from dying?"

³⁸And again Jesus was moved with deep anger. Then they came to the tomb. It was a cave with a heavy stone rolled across its door.

³⁹"Roll the stone aside," Jesus told them.

But Martha, the dead man's sister, said, "By now the smell will be terrible, for he has been dead four days."

⁴⁰"But didn't I tell you that you will see a wonderful miracle from God if you believe?" Jesus asked her.

⁴¹So they rolled the stone aside. Then Jesus looked up to heaven and said, "Father, thank You for hearing Me. ⁴²(You always hear Me, of course, but I said it because of all these people standing here, so that they will believe You sent Me.)"

⁴³Then He shouted, "Lazarus, come out!"

⁴⁴And Lazarus came—bound up in the gravecloth, his face muffled in a head swath. Jesus told them, "Unwrap him and let him go!"

⁴⁵And so at last many of the Jewish leaders who were with Mary and saw it happen, finally believed on Him! ⁴⁶But some went away to the Pharisees and reported it to them. ⁴⁷Then the chief priests and Pharisees convened a council to discuss the situation. "What are we going to do?" they asked each other, "for this man certainly does miracles. ⁴⁸If we let him alone, the whole nation will follow him—and then the Roman army will come and kill us and take over the Jewish government."

⁴⁹But one of them, Caiaphas, who was High Priest that year, said, "You stupid idiots—⁵⁰Let this one man

die for the people—why should the whole nation perish?" ⁵¹This prophecy that Jesus should die for the entire nation came from Caiaphas in his position as High Priest—he didn't think of it by himself, but was inspired to say it. ⁵²It was a prediction that Jesus' death would not be for Israel only, but for all the children of God scattered around the world. ⁵³So from that time on the Jewish leaders began plotting Jesus' death. ⁵⁴Jesus now stopped His public ministry and left Jerusalem; He went to the edge of the desert to the village of Ephraim and stayed there with His disciples. ⁵⁵The Passover, a Jewish holy day, was near, and many country people arrived in Jerusalem several days early so that they could go through the cleansing ceremony before the Passover began. ⁵⁶They wanted to see Jesus, and as they gossiped in the Temple, they asked each other, "What do you think? Will He come for the Passover?"

⁵⁷Meanwhile the chief priests and Pharisees had publicly announced that anyone seeing Jesus must report him immediately so that they could arrest him.

"Miles to go before I sleep . . ."

The miraculous story of the raising of Lazarus is summed up in one sentence uttered by Jesus: "Anyone who believes in Me, even though he dies like anyone else, shall live again." This is indeed how a Christian can be sure he will go to heaven. When a Christian places his confidence in God's Word, he has the promise of Christ Himself that he will live again—eternally. Does it work? Can trust in this promise take you right up to death's door unafraid and still sure of where you are going?

Those who knew Pam McGinley know that it's true. Pam died of leukemia in a Glendale, Calif. hospital three months after being stricken. But before she entered the presence of Christ, she lived a radiant witness for Him that profoundly influenced hundreds, if not thousands, of people.

An adopted child at birth, Pam had a mother who introduced her to the Bible at an early age. When Pam was seven, her mother died—of cancer. Eventually Pam moved in with her aunt and uncle who continued to bring her to Sunday School and church. In seventh grade Pam received Christ as her personal Saviour at a summer camp.

In the fall of 1962 Pam entered high school and her first journalism class assignment was an autobiographic essay. She received an "A" for "Miles to Go Before I Sleep." Prophetically, she wrote:

Today I am waiting ... for the Lord to direct me into a vocation. At the moment I feel called to serve on the mission field. Now—I will live God's life for me. My motto is ... "The woods are lovely, dark and deep, but I have promises to keep, and miles to go before I sleep."*

A week later Pam became quite ill and blood tests revealed she had leukemia. On October 1 the local paper carried her story with a banner headline on page 1. It began with her personally written prayer:

Oh, God, just to dedicate my soul and mind to Thy purpose was not enough. Now You ask for my body. Lord, here I am. If my period of service is up, I willingly come. Here is my body, my physical life, Father, if Thou wilt take me. And if I am to stay here—Thy will be done ...

Pam responded to treatment and was able to go home in a few weeks, but doctors gave her only months to live. On October 28 she spoke to a group of teen-agers at her church and said:

... The key to life, death, and everlasting life is communication—prayer—between man and God, his creator.

Only through prayer have I been given God's strength to accept this situation. I know now what it means to pray without ceasing.

*Pam read these lines in *Deliver Us from Evil* by Dr. Thomas A. Dooley. They are from the 4th stanza of Robert Frost's "Stopping by Woods on a Snowy Evening."

A few weeks later Pam's condition worsened. In the early morning hours of December 18 she dictated these thoughts which were also carried in the local paper:

Since I have known that I have leukemia . . . many people have asked me, "How can you be so happy, knowing that tomorrow may bring death?" From the cards and letters I receive, I know that . . . many think that I am "brave," but I am not. To put it in language familiar to others my age, I'm really a chicken! Without God's hand guiding me, I am weak, afraid and unhappy.

When the doctor first told me that I had leukemia, I was full of doubts, afraid and very unhappy. Then a few hours after I had entered the hospital, I recalled a verse I had memorized as a small child which tells us that God does not give us anything too hard to bear.* I was proud to know that God had made me strong enough to carry this burden. It was an assignment from God, and His confidence in me was rewarding.

. . . I asked Him to become my partner and to make me His disciple that I might witness to those I come in contact with in such a way that I would leave His great message of love and power behind me.

Therefore, we, God and I, set about to shine in the midst of trials. He gave me the only happiness a human can know. There is nothing like it and only those who have established such a partnership with the Lord, and gained His happiness, can know what I mean. Walking hand in hand with God is the only path to human happiness.

Later that same day Pam—now almost blind—scrawled a final message as her aunt held the writing pad:

Both are very much the same—birth and death. Each is the beginning of a new adventure; neither is to be feared; both are beginnings; both hold the Lord's promises. Our first death holds the promise of everlasting life, so it, too, is a birth, into God's kingdom.

The next day Pam McGinley met her Lord face to face. She had wanted to be a missionary, and she was. She traveled far before she slept, and she kept her promise to be a witness for Christ.**

*I Cor. 10:13.
**The story of Pam McGinley adapted from the article, "Miles to Go Before I Sleep . . ." which first appeared in TEACH magazine, Spring 1964. The article was later reproduced as a pamphlet by members of the Junior and Senior High Departments of Glendale Presbyterian Church, Glendale, Calif.

¹Six days before the Passover ceremonies began, Jesus arrived in Bethany where Lazarus was—the man He had brought back to life. ²A banquet was prepared in Jesus' honor. Martha served, and Lazarus sat at the table with Him. ³Then Mary took a jar of costly perfume made from essence of nard, and anointed Jesus' feet with it and wiped them with her hair. And the house was filled with fragrance. ⁴But Judas Iscariot, one of His disciples—the one who would betray Him—said, ⁵"That perfume was worth a fortune! It should have been sold and the money given to the poor!"

⁶Not that he cared for the poor, but he was in charge of the disciples' funds and often dipped into them for his own use!

⁷Jesus replied, "Let her alone. She did it in preparation for My burial. ⁸You can always help the poor, but I won't be with you very long!"

⁹When the ordinary people of Jerusalem heard of His arrival, they flocked to see Him and also to see Lazarus—the man who had come back to life again. ¹⁰Then the chief priests decided to kill Lazarus too, ¹¹For it was because of him that many of the Jewish leaders had deserted and believed in Jesus as their Messiah.

¹²The next day, the news that Jesus was on the way to Jerusalem swept through the city, and a huge crowd of Passover visitors ¹³took palm branches and went down the road to meet him, shouting, "The Savior! God bless the King of Israel! Hail to God's Ambassador!"

¹⁴Jesus rode along on a young donkey, fulfilling the prophecy that said,

¹⁵"Don't be afraid of your King, people of Israel, for He will come to you meekly, sitting on a donkey's colt!"

¹⁶(His disciples didn't realize at the time that this was a fulfillment of prophecy; but after Jesus returned to His glory in heaven, then they noticed how many prophecies of Scripture had come true before their eyes.)

¹⁷And those in the crowd who had seen Jesus call

Lazarus back to life were telling all about it. ¹⁸That was the main reason why so many went out to meet Him—because they had heard about this mighty miracle. ¹⁹Then the Pharisees said to each other, "We've lost. Look—the whole world has gone after him!"

²⁰Some Greeks who had come to Jerusalem to attend the Passover ²¹Paid a visit to Philip,ᵈ who was from Bethsaida, and said, "Sir, we want to meet Jesus."

²²Philip told Andrew about it, and they went together to ask Jesus.

²³,²⁴Jesus replied that the time had come for Him to return to His glory in heaven, and that "I must fall and die like a kernel of wheat that falls between the furrows of the earth. Unless I die I will be alone—a single seed. But My death will produce many new wheat kernels—a plentiful harvest of new lives. ²⁵If you love your life down here—you will lose it. If you despise your life down here—you will exchange it for eternal glory. ²⁶If these Greeksᵉ want to be My disciples, tell them to come and follow Me, for My servants must be where I am. And if they follow Me, the Father will honor them.

²⁷Now My soul is deeply troubled. Shall I pray, 'Father, save Me from what lies ahead'? But that is the very reason why I came! ²⁸Father, bring glory and honor to Your name."

Then a voice spoke from heaven saying, "I have already done this, and I will do it again."

²⁹When the crowd heard the voice, some of them thought it was thunder while others declared an angel had spoken to Him.

³⁰Then Jesus told them, "The voice was for your benefit, not Mine. ³¹The time of judgment for the world has come—and the time when Satan,ᶠ the prince of this world, shall be cast out. ³²And when I am lifted up [on the crossᵍ], I will draw everyone to Me." ³³He said this to indicate how He was going to die.

³⁴"Die?" asked the crowd. "We understood that the Messiah would live forever and never die. Why are

you saying He will die? What Messiah are you talking about?"

[35]Jesus replied, "My light will shine out for you just a little while longer. Walk in it while you can, and go where you want to go before the darkness falls, for then it will be too late for you to find your way. [36]Make use of the Light while there is still time; then you will become light bearers."[h]

After saying these things, Jesus went away and was hidden from them. [37]But despite all the miracles He had done, most of the people would not believe He was the Messiah. [38]This is exactly what Isaiah the prophet had predicted:

"Lord, who will believe us? Who will accept God's mighty miracles as proof?"[i]

[39]But they couldn't believe, for as Isaiah also said:

[40]"God[j] has blinded their eyes and hardened their hearts so that they can neither see nor understand nor turn to Me to heal them."

[41]Isaiah was referring to Jesus when he made this prediction, for he had seen a vision of the Messiah's glory. [42]However, even many of the Jewish leaders believed Him to be the Messiah but wouldn't admit it to anyone because of their fear that the Pharisees would excommunicate them from the synagogue; [43]For they loved the praise of men more than the praise of God.

[44]Jesus shouted to the crowds, "If you trust Me, you are really trusting God. [45]For when you see Me, you are seeing the one who sent Me. [46]I have come as a Light to shine in this dark world, so that all who put their trust in Me will no longer wander in the darkness. [47]If anyone hears Me and doesn't obey Me, I am not his judge—for I have come to save the world and not to judge it. [48]But all who reject Me and My message will be judged at the Day of Judgment by the truths I have spoken. [49]For these are not My own ideas, but I have told you what the Father said to tell you. [50]And

129

I know His instructions give eternal life; so whatever He tells Me to say, I say!"

Forty brave soldiers for Christ

Today, Palm Sunday sermons usually stress that Jesus' entry into Jerusalem was a time of triumph and great honor. But, have you ever considered that when Jesus rode into Jerusalem on the back of an ass He had already been branded an outlaw? Jesus' entry into Jerusalem is an example of supreme courage, not a coronation. It is an example to give Christians of every age inspiration to be witnesses for Him no matter what happens.

Stories of the Christian martyrs who were thrown to the wild beasts and burned at stakes during the Roman persecutions are well known. But a story that is not so well known was the persecution of 40 Roman soldiers—all Christians who died a slow and grisly death because they would not bow to Caesar and call him their God.

Forty good soldiers for Christ they were, and the pride of the Roman Empire. All were from Cappadocia, and all were members of the vaunted Twelfth, or "Thundering," Legion in Rome's imperial army.

It was mid-winter, A.D. 320, and the 40 Cappadocian warriors were stationed with the Twelfth Legion at Sabaste, a city of Lesser Armenia south of the Black Sea. Reigning as Caesar in the eastern portion at that time was Valerius Licinius, who began to grow increasingly hostile toward Christians because the Christian emperor of the western portion of the Roman Empire, Constantine, was increasing in strength and threatening Licinius' territory.

Licinius "cracked down" on the Christians in his territory and issued the order that all civil servants had to offer sacrifice on pagan altars before the local deities. "Civil servants" meant all members of the Roman army. So the Twelfth Legion heard the order given by their captain, Agricolas. Shortly afterward, a spokesman for the 40 Cappadocians came to Agricolas' tent and told him that there were 40 Christians in his ranks who would not go through with the ritual of sacrifice. The 40 soldiers were confined to military prison and later brought to trial for court martial.

Agricolas opened formalities by saying, "Of all the soldiers who serve the Emperor, none are more intelligent than you, none are more effective in military operations, none more loved by us and none more needed right now. Do not turn our love into hatred. It lies in you whether to be loved or hated."

Kandidos, one of the spokesmen for the 40, replied "we have made our choice. We shall devote our love to our God."

Because he did not have authority to sentence the Christians to death, Agricolas had to wait for the arrival of general Lysias, who would be making an inspection of the Twelfth Legion in about a week.

The Christians were put in the custody of the jailer, Aglaios, to await the arrival of the general.

A week later Lysias came, agreed with the opinions of captain Agricolas, and gave the Christians the alternative to obey the imperial order to sacrifice to pagan deities or be delivered over for torture.

Kandidos replied for all 40 and said, "You can have our armor, and our bodies as well. We prefer Christ."

Next morning the soldiers heard their sentence. They were to be bound, ropes placed around their necks and led to the shore of a nearby frozen lake where at sundown they were to be stripped and marched to the middle of the ice. At any time, they could still recant and find refuge in a heated bathhouse on the lakeshore.

Aglaios, the jailer who had been caring for the men for a week watched as the 40 soldiers were stripped and marched, shivering into the dusk. Guards were posted all around the shore to make sure they did not try to escape.

One of the band struck a song: "Forty good soldiers for Christ!

"We shall not depart from You as long as You give us life. . . ."

The men took heart, but as the hour of midnight approached their sounds grew more feeble. Then, one of the 40 was seen emerging from the darkness of the lake. He fell to his knees on shore and began crawling toward the bathhouse. Only the jailer, Aglaios, was awake and he heard a thin quavering cry, "Thirty-nine good soldiers for Christ!" Aglaios watched the man enter the bathhouse and emerge quickly, apparently overcome by the heat. He saw the man collapse to the ground and lie still.

At that moment something happened in the heart of Aglaios the jailer. What it was, only he and God will ever know; the guards reported hearing a great shout, jerking them awake. Rubbing their eyes, they watched him wrench off his armor and girdle and dash to the edge of the lake. There, after lifting his right hand and crying, "Forty good soldiers for Christ!" he disappeared over the ice and into the darkness.

Next morning captain Agricolas ordered the victims brought to shore. They were found frozen in the middle of the ice. Many wept openly as the bodies were loaded into waiting chariots by fellow legionnaires. Suddenly, captain Agricolas saw the body of Aglaios the jailer. "What is he doing there?" he demanded.

"We cannot understand it, Captain," replied one of the guards. "It was far into the night, when all of a sudden he jumped to his feet, shouted something, stripped off his armor and ran. We could not get near him to stop him."

"Was he bewitched?"

"Probably, sire. Ever since those Christians came under his care, we noticed something different about him. At times he would be singing under his breath. It was a bad sign, we decided. Too much music is bad for soldiers. Makes them queer, don't you think so, Captain?"*

*The story of the "Forty Martyrs of Sebaste" is adapted from the account in *Decision*, December 1963. It comes from an ancient Greek account first published in German in 1902 and especially translated for *Decision*.

TAKE TIME...

Emergency call from Bethany. Read John 11:1-16. Why does Jesus seem to "stall" after receiving word of Lazarus' illness? See especially verse 4.

Believe in Me and never die. Read John 11:17-27. What does Jesus' claim to be the "Resurrection and the Life" mean to you personally?

Lazarus, come forth! Why do you think Jesus did this particular miracle? What was He trying to teach His followers? What does this miracle teach you?

Jesus becomes an outlaw. Read John 11:45-57. What are the motives behind the Pharisees' decision to do away with Jesus? Are they similar to motives that people have today when they "do away with Jesus." Make a comparison and see.

Your King is coming! Compare John 12:12-19 with Zech. 9:9. Jesus is fulfilling messianic prophecy as He rides into Jerusalem amidst a cheering throng. Do you think the people are cheering for the right reason? Why? Why not?

Hate your life to keep it. Read John 12:20-26. What does Jesus mean when He says to love your life means losing it and to hate your life means keeping it for eternity? What do verses 24-26 have to say about "telling it like it is" concerning Jesus Christ?

The reluctant witnesses. Read John 12:42,43. Why did the "authorities" who believed in Jesus remain silent? Why is it easy to fall into the trap of loving the praise of men more than the praise of God?

TAKE INVENTORY...

Review the story of Pam McGinley, high school student who had died of leukemia. If you faced the same kind of death, do you think you could be as happy and confident in Christ?

When Jesus rode into Jerusalem, it was an act of supreme courage, of selfless sacrifice for the love of others. In what ways have you been a courageous Christian lately? (Keep in mind that courage doesn't always mean physical bravery.) In what ways could you be more courageous in your stand for Christ?

TAKE ACTION ...

Do something to testify for Christ this week that—for you—will take a great deal of courage. Pray for courage to do it and trust God to take care of the rest.

CHAPTER 12

An impossible order?

What is humility?

Confucius said it is the solid foundation of all virtues.

Charles Spurgeon, one of the great preachers of all time, said humility is to make a right estimate of yourself.

Philosopher John Ruskin said that he believed that the first test of the truly great man is his humility.

Ivan Miller, a lawyer, had this thought: "Humility is such a frail and delicate thing that he who dares to think that he has it proves that he does not."

And as the great philosopher Montaigne observed: "One may be humble out of pride."

It would seem humility is not easy to describe or define. Perhaps it is easier to watch humility in action...

John 13:1-20

[1,2,3]Jesus knew on the evening of Passover Day that it would be His last night on earth before returning to His Father. During supper the Devil had already suggested to Judas Iscariot, Simon's son, that this was the night to carry out his plan to betray Jesus. Jesus knew that the Father had given Him everything and that He had come from God and would return to God. And how He loved His disciples! [4]So He got up from the supper table, took off His robe, wrapped a towel around His loins,[k] [5]poured water into a basin, and began to wash the disciples' feet and to wipe them with the towel He had around Him.

[6]When He came to Simon Peter, Peter said to Him, "Master, You shouldn't be washing our feet like this!"

[7]Jesus replied, "You don't understand now why I am doing it; some day you will."

[8]"No," Peter protested, "You shall never wash my feet!"

"But if I don't, you can't be My partner," Jesus replied.

[9]Simon Peter exclaimed, "Then wash my hands and head as well—not just my feet!"

[10]Jesus replied, "One who has bathed all over needs only to have his feet washed to be entirely clean. Now you are clean—but that isn't true of everyone here."

[11]For Jesus knew who would betray Him. That is what He meant when He said, "Not all of you are clean."

[12]After washing their feet He put on His robe again and sat down and asked, "Do you understand what I was doing? [13]You call Me 'Master' and 'Lord,' and you do well to say it, for it is true. [14]And since I, the Lord and Teacher, have washed your feet, you ought to wash each other's feet. [15]I have given you an example to follow: do as I have done to you. [16]How true it is that a servant is not greater than his master! Nor is the messenger more important than the one

who sends him. ¹⁷You know these things—now do them! That is the path of blessing.

¹⁸"I am not saying these things to all of you; I know so well each one of you I chose. The Scripture declares,

" 'One who eats supper with Me will betray Me,' and this will soon come true. ¹⁹I tell you this now so that when it happens, you will believe on Me. ²⁰Truly, anyone welcoming the Holy Spirit, whom I will send, is welcoming Me. And to welcome Me is to welcome the Father who sent Me."

Humility is love in action

Various interpretations of Christ's washing of the disciples' feet are made. Some churches find within this act deep theological significance; others see it as a simple lesson that defines humility as service to others.*

When Jesus did this most inferior of acts, He was certainly saying that humility is the absence of pride. Jesus was saying that humility is not only "putting pride in your pocket"; it is getting down on your knees—physically (if necessary) and psychologically (which is often hardest to do).

Jesus told His disciples that He had done this as an example and that they should do it also. What does this mean for a Christian today? How can the Christian show humility? More important, how can the Christian be humble without being proud about it or disgustingly self-depreciating in a phony kind of way?

Perhaps one way to think of some practical in-

*Some congregations explain foot washing as an ordinance instituted by Christ to be practiced and perpetuated by the church. Washing of the feet symbolizes a great spiritual truth, namely, the cleansing of the daily walk of the believer by the application of the Word of God.

PRIDE AND HUMILITY DON'T MIX

terpretations of humility is to think of choices we all face every day. For example:

You face the choice of telling a friend, someone in your family, or a teacher, that you were wrong and that you are sorry, or you can maintain proud silence.

You face the choice of "saying hello first" in the hall or on the street, or you can look the other way and decide "some people are awfully stuck up."

Someone asks you to do something for them when it looks to you as if he could just as well do it himself. You can go ahead and do it or you can say, "Who was your servant last year?"

There are endless possibilities. At the bottom of every one of them, however, is one basic choice: To put yourself ahead of or behind others, to worry about others first or worry about "number one" first.

But it isn't natural to think about others first. We

139

all face situations where we know that we should be humble and put ourselves second, but if we are honest we admit that we really don't want to. Perhaps, as Jesus points out in the next scene at the last supper, one thing more is still needful...

John 13:21-38

[21]Now Jesus was in great anguish of spirit and exclaimed, "Yes, it is true—one of you will betray Me."

[22]The disciples looked at each other wondering whom He could mean. [23]Since I[m] was sitting next[n] to Jesus at the table, being His closest friend, [24]Simon Peter motioned to me to ask Him who it was who would do this terrible deed.

[25]So I turned[o] and asked Him, "Lord, who is it?"

[26]He told me, "It is the one I honor by giving the bread dipped in the sauce."[p]

And when He had dipped it, He gave it to Judas, son of Simon Iscariot. [27]As soon as Judas had eaten it, Satan entered into him. Then Jesus told him, "Hurry—do it now."

[28]None of the others at the table knew what Jesus meant. [29]Some thought that since Judas was their treasurer, Jesus was telling him to go and pay for the food or to give some money to the poor. [30]Judas left at once, going out into the night.

[31]As soon as Judas left the room, Jesus said, "My time has come; the glory of God will soon surround Me—and God shall receive great praise because of all that happens to Me. [32]And God shall give Me His own glory, and this so very soon. [33]Dear, dear children, how brief are these moments before I must go away and leave you! Then, though you search for Me, you cannot come to Me—just as I told the Jewish leaders. [34]And so I am giving a new commandment to you now—love each other just as much as I love you. [35]Your strong love for each other will prove to the world that you are My disciples."

³⁶Simon Peter said, "Master, where are You going?" And Jesus replied, "You can't go with Me now; but you will follow Me later."

³⁷"But why can't I come now?" he asked, "for I am ready to die for You."

³⁸Jesus answered, "Die for Me? No—three times before the cock crows tomorrow morning, you will deny that you even know Me!"

A "new" commandment?

The next few moments must have been terribly painful for Jesus. He had shown His disciples an act of loving humility and Judas repaid Him by rejecting Jesus' final offer to abandon his plans to betray Him. Was Judas too proud? Perhaps. At any rate, he went out into the night to betray his Lord and to do it quickly.

And then Jesus turns to His disciples and gives them a new commandment. A new commandment? What is new about loving one another? Does not the Old Testament tell men to love their neighbors as themselves? Yes, but Jesus added one condition for it: ". . . love each other just *as much as I love you*" (v. 34).

Jesus is saying that humility is a coin with two sides. The other side—the side that should be face up—is love. As Christians love one another there is less room for pride, less chance for pious pretense. Love makes it possible to do the menial, the dirty, the inferior, the filthy task. Love and pride simply do not mix. To try to be "humble" is impossible. But as you love others just as much as Christ loved you, the humility will show itself.

But just how do you learn to love others as Christ

141

has loved you? What is involved? Fierce determination such as Peter showed when he said that he'd follow Christ to the death (v. 37)?

Jesus' answer to Peter is His answer to us, if we think we are going to love in our own strength. Die for Christ? We will not die for Him, nor will we communicate Him as long as we think we can follow Him by counting on our own "noble determination." That kind of love is based on pride, and proud people find the commandment to love others as Christ has loved them impossible indeed. There must be more to being a Christian than this ... and there is. Christ tells His disciples about it in one of the most encouraging passages in all Scripture...

John 14:1-11

[1]"Let not your heart be troubled. You are trusting God, now trust in Me.

[2,3]"There are many homes up there where My Father lives, and I am going to prepare them for your coming. When everything is ready then I will come and get you, so that you can always be with Me where I am. If this weren't so, I would tell you plainly. [4]And you know where I am going and how to get there."

[5]"No, we don't," Thomas said. "We haven't any idea where You are going, so how can we know the way?"

[6]Jesus told him, "I am the Way—yes, and the Truth and the Life. No one can get to the Father except by means of Me. [7]If you had known who I am, then you would have known who My Father is. From now on you know Him—and have seen Him!"

[8]Philip said, "Sir, show us the Father and we will be satisfied."

[9]Jesus replied, "Don't you even yet know who I am, Philip, even after all this time I have been with you? Anyone who has seen Me has seen the Father! So why

are you asking to see Him? [20]Don't you believe that I am in the Father and the Father is in Me? The words I say are not My own but are from My Father who lives in Me. And He does His work through Me. [21]Just believe it—that I am in the Father and the Father is in Me. Or else believe it because of the mighty miracles you have seen Me do."

It's out of your hands

These verses contain two key ideas. First, Jesus tells His disciples that if they want to learn how to love in humility they must trust and believe in Him and then be willing to back up their profession with positive action. For example, you might say that for "Christ's sake" you would be willing to go help clean out a cesspool at a church camp. But your words would have little meaning unless you really got down in that cesspool and worked with the others in the stench and the mess.

Second, the reason Jesus' disciples can confidently trust in Him is that He is God Himself. He is the way, the truth and the life. They have seen the Father.

In other words, when it comes to living the Christian life, when it comes to communicating Christ to others, when it comes to loving one another as Christ loves you, when it comes to following Christ's example of humility, the matter is really not in your hands but in God's. You have to come to a place where you see that you can't "try" to do these things. You can only trust Christ—put your life under His control.

This kind of trust empowered George Mueller to

found an orphanage on faith with no money in the bank and no visible means of gaining any. Mueller's orphanage was run according to the following rules:

He never solicited funds, nor did he ever reveal facts or figures concerning the needs of the orphanage to anyone except God in prayer.

He never incurred any debts because he did not want to be a burden on local shop keepers or suppliers.

If money was contributed for a specific purpose it was always used for that purpose (in other words, funds were never converted to pay a certain bill or buy food if they were earmarked for a specific use by a giver to the orphanage).

Professional auditors checked all accounts annually. All donors were thanked in private and their names were never published along with the size of their gifts. Mueller didn't try to get prominent or important people on his board as a means of publicity or advertising.

Instead of spending time in fund raising, Mueller spent hours in prayer. Before he was through, he had built five new orphanage buildings, added over 100 people to his staff, and cared for more than 2,000 orphans. All in all, George Mueller handled over $7,000,000 for God in his lifetime in one of the most remarkable demonstrations of depending entirely upon God the world has ever seen.

George Mueller was one example of the fulfillment of the very next promise Christ makes His disciples. . .

John 14:12-14

[12,13]"In solemn truth I tell you, anyone believing in Me shall do the same miracles I have done, and even greater ones, because I am going to be with the Father. You can ask Him for *anything*, using My name, and I will do it, for this will bring praise to the Father because of what I, the Son, will do for you. [14]Yes, ask *anything* using My name, and I will do it!"

A "blank check" from the Bank of Heaven?

Taken out of its context, these words can be misleading. It sounds like Jesus is giving His disciples a "blank check," that all they have to do is pray and they will get what they want. But the key here is not that they will get whatever *they* want, the key is that they must pray in Christ's name, and to pray in Christ's name means to seek God's will, not yours. George Mueller sought God's will and God answered his prayers in incredible, uncanny ways. But then why be surprised when God works in an uncanny way? He has been doing it for centuries as He carries out Jesus' promise that His disciples would do even greater works than He has done (v. 13).

Take, for example, the story of the five martyred missionaries who were speared to death by Auca Indians in 1956. It was a tragedy that startled and horrified the entire world. Many people talked of the needless waste of these young lives and the needless risks they took to try to take the Gospel to stone age Indians deep in the jungles of Ecuador.

Yet, ten years afterward, the Gospel was among these Indians—taken there by Rachel Saint and Betty Elliot, widows of two of the five martyrs.

With humility and love that could come only through complete trust in Christ, these women succeeded in making contact with the Auca's and even winning some of their husbands' murderers to Christ.* Rachel Saint, Betty Elliot and George Mueller are only three of a line of countless Christians who have learned the meaning of trusting Christ as well as learning the meaning of another command that He first gave on that night of the last supper. . .

John 14:15-24

[15,16]"If you love Me, obey Me; and I will ask the Father and He will give you another Comforter, and He will never leave you. [17]He is the Holy Spirit who leads into all truth. The world at large cannot receive Him, for it isn't looking for Him and doesn't recognize Him. But you do, for He lives with you now and some day shall be in you. [18]No, I will not abandon you or leave you as orphans in the storm—I will come to you. [19]In just a little while I will be gone from the world, but I will still be present with you. For I will live again—and you will too. [20]When I come back to life again, you will know that I am in My Father, and you in Me, and I in you.

[21]"The one who obeys Me is the one who loves Me, and because he loves Me, My Father will love him; and I will too, and I will reveal Myself to him."

[22]Judas (not Judas Iscariot, but His other disciple with that name) said to Him, "Sir, why are You going to reveal Yourself only to us disciples and not to the world at large?"

[23]Jesus replied, "Because I will only reveal Myself to those who love Me and obey Me. The Father will love them too, and We will come to them and

*See "Ten Years after the Massacre," Rachel Saint, *Decision*, January, 1966.

live with them. 24Anyone who doesn't obey Me doesn't love Me. And remember, I am not making up this answer to your question! It is the answer given by the Father who sent Me."

How to avoid spiritual vertigo

Have you ever heard of "vertigo"? Former fighter pilot Lane Adams, who later went into the ministry and then joined the staff of the Billy Graham evangelistic team, had a narrow squeak when flying a mission during World War II because his wing man got vertigo.

Adams was flying with his squadron in particularly heavy weather off Okinawa. His mission was to find a Japanese kamikaze plane that had been circling the fleet. Everyone was on instruments because of the heavy cloud cover, and the only hope to find the kamikaze pilot was to try to run across him in small half-mile openings in the clouds.

Suddenly, Adams noticed that he was losing air speed. He checked his altimeter and saw that he and his wing man were gaining altitude and in a "nose-high" attitude. He peered across at the other pilot who seemed to be all right, but then Adams realized that they were both going so dangerously slow that their collision was almost imminent. Adams threw on full power and zoomed by the other plane to safety.

Back on the carrier he asked the other pilot what had happened. The other man said that he was under the impression that his plane was going straight and level. He had been unaware that he

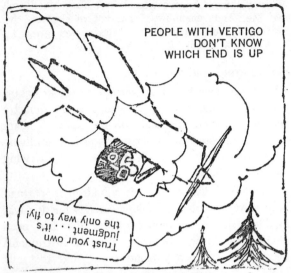

had been climbing and slowing down to almost a stall condition that would have thrown him into a spin and back into Adams' plane.

The pilot flying with Adams had suffered an attack of vertigo, which is defined in aeronautical terms as an "error or illusion of spacial orientations, an experience in which the pilot is confused about his relationship to the earth or to other objects in the sky." In other words, the pilot doesn't know which end is up. Birds can also get vertigo as can ballet dancers and even Eskimos in kayaks.

How does a pilot avoid vertigo—the condition that has sent many of them to their deaths in graveyard spins? Adams writes that when a pilot is taught to fly on instruments, he has one thing drummed into him: "When you get into the clouds

148

and lose visual reference to the ground, forget everything you think, forget everything you feel. Concentrate on what those instruments tell you. Believe them, and correct your flight accordingly."

The key here, then, for a pilot in an instrument flight situation is to *obey his instruments. He is to trust them; do exactly what they tell him.*

The application to the spiritual realm isn't too hard to make here. Many Christians have "spiritual vertigo" because they get into situations where they don't really trust and obey. Ironically enough, they have far more than instruments to guide them. They have a Command Pilot—the Holy Spirit of Christ, who is promised to all believers in John 14:16,17. As v. 18 says, Christ will not leave His disciples like orphans in a storm, (or like instrumentless pilots in a cloud bank). He gives them guidance and keeps them well aware of which end is up if they will trust Him and obey Him.

Just how do you trust and obey? How do you know when the Holy Spirit is giving you a certain bearing on your instruments?

The first thing (the thing many Christians don't do) is to realize that the following Proverb is most correct: "Trust in the Lord with all thine heart; and lean not unto thine own understanding. In all thy ways acknowledge him, and he shall direct thy paths" (Proverbs 3:5,6). In all too many situations, especially situations that involve communicating Christ, Christians get spiritual vertigo because they aren't basically committed to the idea that they will trust Christ and not themselves; that even though they can't see through the cloud bank, they will depend on Him and nothing else. To depend on Him, brings a Christian an all-important "by-product" that makes him a still more effective witness...

John 14:25-31

[25]"I am telling you these things now while I am still with you. [26]But when the Father sends the Comforter[q] to represent Me[r]—and by the Comforter I mean the Holy Spirit—He will teach you much, as well as remind you of everything I Myself have told you.

[27]"I am leaving you with a gift—peace of mind and heart! And the peace I give isn't fragile like the peace the world gives. So don't be troubled or afraid.[s] [28]Remember what I told you—I am going away, but I will come back to you again. If you really love Me, you will be very happy for Me, for now I can go to the Father, who is greater than I am. [29]I have told you these things before they happen so that when they do, you will believe [in Me[t]]. [30]I don't have much more time to talk to you, for the evil prince of this world approaches. He has no power over Me. [31]But I will freely do what the Father requires of Me so that the world will know that I love the Father. Come, let's be going."

Peace despite an executioner's sword

To the Christian who trusts and obeys Him, Christ leaves a gift—peace of mind and heart, peace that isn't fragile like the "tranquility" that the world seeks for its jangled nerves. There are times in life when peace has to mean more than relief from Excedrin headaches.

From the famous book, *Through the Valley of the Kwai* by Ernest Gordon, comes this incident which describes the kind of peace that only Christ

PEACE DESPITE AN EXECUTIONER'S SWORD

can give—but remember that it is peace that comes through trust and obedience, not in a bottle.

"An Aussie private had been caught outside the fence while trying to obtain medicine from the Thais for his sick friends. He was summarily tried and sentenced to death (by the Japanese prison authorities).

On the morning set for his execution he marched cheerfully along between his guards to the parade ground. The Japanese were out in full force to observe the scene. The Aussie was permitted to have his commanding officer and a chaplain in attendance as witnesses. The party came to a halt. The C.O. and the chaplain were waved to one side. The Aussie was left standing alone.

Calmly, he surveyed his executioners. Then he

drew a small copy of the New Testament from a pocket of his ragged shorts. He read a passage unhurriedly to himself. His lips moved but no sound came from them.

What that passage was, no one will ever know. I cannot help wondering, however, if it was not those words addressed by Jesus to His disciples in the Upper Room:

Let not your heart be troubled:
Ye believe in God, believe also in me.
In my Father's house are many mansions:
If it were not so, I would have told you.
I go to prepare a place for you.
And if I go and prepare a place for you,
I will come again, and receive you unto myself;
That where I am, there ye may be also.
. . . Peace I leave with you,
My peace I give unto you;
Not as the world giveth, give I unto you.
Let not your heart be troubled,
Neither let it be afraid.

He finished reading, returned his New Testament to his pocket, looked up, and saw the agitated face of his chaplain. He smiled, waved to him, and called out,

"Cheer up, Padre. It isn't as bad as all that. I'll be all right."

He nodded to his executioner as a sign that he was ready. Then he knelt down, and bent his head forward to expose his neck.

The Samurai sword flashed in the sunlight.*

*From *The Valley of the Kwai,* Ernest Gordon. Copyright 1962. Harper and Row Publishers. Used by permission.

TAKE TIME . . .

What kind of an act is this? Read John 13:1-20. The scene is the last supper. Jesus knows that tomorrow He will die. He has many things to tell His disciples. Why does He choose to wash their feet? What is He trying to tell them as He does this act?

Do your dirty work quickly. Read John 13:21-30. Up to the last moment, Jesus gave Judas a chance to change his mind. Write down what you believe were the basic reasons why Judas decided to go through with the most infamous act in all history.

Is this legislated love? Read John 13:31-38. Why do you think Jesus tells His disciples that He is giving them a "new commandment" to love one another? Is it fair for Christ to "command" us to love one another? Why? Why not?

Do you really know who He is? Read John 14:1-11. In verses 1-4, Jesus offers the disciples encouragement, but they remain puzzled. What do they still seem to lack? (See especially vs. 5 and 8.) Is this what many Christians still lack today? If so, why?

Is prayer a "blank check"? Read John 14:12-14. Is Jesus offering His disciples a "blank check" or are there conditions here? What does it mean to ask something in Jesus' name? Can you ask for *anything* in Christ's name? Why? Why not?

You say you love Christ? Read John 14:15-24. Christians often talk about their "love for Christ" but what do these verses tell you that goes beyond mere talk? How do you prove your love for Christ and gain the power He can send through the Holy Spirit? What connection do you see between this passage and John 13:34,35?

Is peace the absence of "war"? Read John 14:25-31. Jesus promises His disciples peace, but not the kind of peace the world offers. Is Jesus promising quiet tranquility? Is that the way life really works? Compare Isaiah 26:3. Is it possible for the Christian to have "peace" in the midst of trouble, trials, strife, even war? Why had it better be possible?

TAKE INVENTORY . . .

Think through your understanding and concept of the key words in this chapter: humility, love, trust, obey, peace. Do you see how they all blend together and that without one you cannot have the others? Which of these elements for an effective Christian witness do you have the most trouble with in your daily experience? For example, do you find it hard to love others? Then examine how much trusting and obeying of Christ you are doing in regard to the person you find it hard to love. Do you worry a lot? Again, you come back to the question: are you trusting and obeying Him? To trust and obey Christ—are two hinges on which the door of every Christian life swings.

TAKE ACTION . . .

Seek out a Christian friend and share with him your ideas about the key words in this chapter: humility, love, trust, obedience, peace. Share together the problems that you have in regard to these virtues. Pray together about some practical plan you can put into action to put trust and obedience to work as you witness to a specific person or perhaps a certain group of people. Think together honestly about how the non-Christians you know see you and how they would recognize genuine trust and obedience in a Christian.

If possible, (and if you have the nerve) talk to one or more non-Christians and ask them point blank if they think that they can see trust and obedience to Christ in your life. If they say they don't, ask them why. The conversation could turn into an excellent opportunity to communicate Christ.

CHAPTER 13

What is a "fruitful" Christian?

"I've worked here for years," said the missionary, "and I've seen hardly any conversions. I'm a failure, a fruitless Christian, and in John 15 I've been reading about what happens to fruitless Christians. They are thrown into the fire and burned."*

Was the missionary right? Was he a fruitless Christian because he had labored on his mission field for years with little "results"? When the Bible speaks of "bearing fruit," is it talking about winning people to Christ?

Is Christian "fruitfulness" to be equated with "successful witnessing"? And what about you? Suppose you have been a Christian for several months

*See "Beyond Success," Eric Fife, *His*, April 1963, p. 5.

or years. Suppose you haven't won anyone to Christ. Are you "fruitless"? Perhaps a review of John 15 is in order. . . .

John 15:1-11

¹"I am the true Vine, and My Father is the Gardener. ²He lops off every branch that doesn't produce, and He prunes those branches that bear fruit for even larger crops. ³He has already tended you by pruning you back for greater strength and usefulness by means of the commands I gave you. ⁴Take care to live in Me, and let Me live in you. For a branch can't produce fruit when severed from the vine. Nor can you

---

Why Jesus talked about "the vine and the branches"

When making a spiritual point, Jesus would often choose a familiar object or idea and his choice of "the vine and the branches and bearing fruit" is no exception. In Israel at that time, the grapevine was the symbol of the nation. Jewish prophets had often referred to Israel as a vine or a vineyard, but when the Old Testament prophets used this analogy they were saying that Israel was like a vineyard that had run wild and gone to seed, it was like a vineyard that was empty and fruitless. But Christ uses this analogy differently. In John 15 He is saying that He is the true vine—that is, the real vine of God. The real vine of God is not a nation or a race (something that many Jews thought was true). The real vine is Jesus Christ, Himself, and all who believe and trust in Him are "branches" on that vine. In this analogy, Jesus also points out that His Father is the "husbandman" or gardener who tends the true vine. The branches of the true vine are pruned (cut back) in order to produce more fruit and not just more wood and leaves. The warning in v. 6 has bothered many Christians. Jesus says that the person who abides (lives) in Christ and lets Christ live in him will be "fruitful", but if a man does not abide in Christ, he will be cast forth as a branch, gathered and thrown into the fire to burn. Does this verse mean that a Christian is lost if he does not "bear fruit" for Christ? Because the context of John 15 is not dealing with salvation, but with a person's relationship to Christ, perhaps it is better to see these words as a warning. The person who claims he is a Christian and gives lip service to Christianity but who does not bear fruit in his life is risking the fate of being a useless and powerless Christian. The point being made here is that as far as the Christian is concerned, without Christ he can do absolutely nothing.

---

be fruitful apart from Me. ⁶Yes, I am the Vine; you are the branches. Whoever lives in Me and I in him shall produce a large crop of fruit. For apart from Me you can't do a thing. ⁶If anyone separates from Me, he is thrown away like a useless branch, withers, and is gathered into a pile with all the others and burned. ⁷But if you stay in Me and obey My commands, you may ask any request you like, and it will be granted! ⁸My true disciples produce bountiful harvests. This brings great glory to My Father.

⁹"I have loved you even as the Father has loved Me. Live within My love. ¹⁰When you obey Me you are living in My love, just as I obey My Father and live in His love. ¹¹I have told you this so that you will be filled with My joy. Yes, your cup of joy will overflow!

The fruit of the Spirit is. . .

There you have it. Jesus plainly says that if we abide in Him (that is, if we share our lives with Him and let Him share His life and power with us) we will "bear much fruit." If fruit is to be equated with souls won for Christ, then the discouraged missionary whom you met at the beginning of this chapter obviously wasn't "abiding in Christ."

But just what is "fruit"? There is no mention in this passage of fruit being equated with conversions. But in Galatians 5:22,23, the "fruit of the Spirit" is clearly described: love, joy, peace, long suffering, gentleness, goodness, meekness, temperance and faith. This is the "fruit" that Christ was talking about when He told his disciples to abide in Him.

The discouraged missionary was wrong. He confused "success" in Christian service with fruitfulness. He mistook Christian soul winning for witnessing. He mistook leading people to Christ for communicating Christ. If we are to equate winning souls with bearing fruit, then Christ Himself had a rather "fruitless" ministry. As far as sheer numbers and popular opinion were concerned, Jesus ended His ministry with far more people against Him than for Him.

In the words of missionary writer Eric Fife, "Fruits of the Spirit are primarily concerned not with service, but with character. They don't necessarily refer to a person's usefulness, but to what he is. Fife points out that we are not all called to be Billy Grahams. We are, however, called to be loving and to have peace and faith.* As the Christian bears the fruit of the Spirit in his life, God uses that kind of fruit to draw others to Him."

So far, so good. The Christian who has not won "a soul a week" need not feel discouraged. On the other hand, he does need to be concerned about how much fruit of the Spirit he is bearing in his life. How does he go about bearing this kind of fruit? Does this idea of bearing fruit put the Christian right back on the treadmill called works and legalism?

Not so. When He gave His disciples this analogy, Jesus was plainly emphasizing a way to stay away from making Christianity nothing but rules and regulations. The key here is "to abide in Christ."

The word "abide" is not used a great deal in casual conversation today. To "abide" means to stay

*See "Beyond Success", Eric Fife, *His*, April 1963, p. 5.

with, to be with, to live with, to share with. To abide means "to be joined to." What Jesus was saying here was that to abide in Him would be difficult to do on the basis of a casual or indifferent relationship. When you really abide with Christ, you are part of Him and He is part of you.

In May of 1962 the world was astounded by the report that doctors had succeeded in sewing back an arm that had been completely cut from a boy's body. Everett Knowles, 12-year-old Little League pitcher living in Sommerville, Mass., had gotten out of school one afternoon and decided to try his luck at a favorite "sport" for kids in Sommerville—to grab a ride on a slowly passing freight as it moved through town.

Everett succeeded in hopping aboard a box car and hanging on the side, but he didn't see the concrete overpass and abutment until it was too late. No one knows exactly how it happened, but apparently, there was no room for Everett's body between the abutment and the freight car. He was knocked from the train and his arm completely severed just below the right shoulder.

Incredibly, the arm stayed inside Everett's shirt and he managed to reach the loading platform of the Handy Card and Paper Company on nearby Medford Street. One of the workers who tried to help Everett was Mrs. Alice Chmielewski. As she tried to make a tourniquet to stop the bleeding she found a gap in Everett's sleeve. His arm wasn't broken; it was completely off! The ambulance rushed up and Everett was taken to the General Hospital in nearby Boston. Doctors quickly examined him, saw that the arm was still in good condition and decided to perform the history-making operation.

The sewing of the important brachial arteries and veins was by far the most crucial step in the operation, because circulation had to be restored to the arm if it were to be useful again. The sewing was supervised by Dr. Robert Shaw who patiently and skillfully made the tiny stitches in the artery and veins, which were only 1/6 of an inch thick. Two hours later, clamps were loosened and blood was allowed to flow into the newly sutured veins. The boy's arm turned from a cold and corpse-like blue-white to warm and pink, and doctors could even feel his pulse in his wrist.

The doctors also faced the formidable task of rejoining the severed humerus bone. For this they used a 6¼" steel rod called a "Kuntscher" nail. Dr. Ronald Malt drove the nail through the narrow cavity of the remaining stump of the humerus bone. Then, while Dr. Lucian Leape held the arm in place, surgeon David Mitchell forced the severed bone onto the free end of the nail by applying pressure with only his hands.

The final major step in the operation—the rejoining of the nerves in the arm—was not completed until several months later and Everett Knowles faced many months of waiting and exercising in order to obtain usefulness and feeling in his arm again.*

The dramatic details involved in "sewing back an

*For accounts of the miraculous operation on Everett Knowles arm, see *Time*, June 8, 1962 and *Popular Science*, November 1962.

arm" can help the Christian better understand the analogy of the vine and the branches. It is easy to understand how an arm must "abide in" the body if it is to get its proper blood supply, if it is to be useful and strong, if it is to have feeling and sensitivity. In the same way, a Christian must abide in Christ. If he does not, his supply of nourishment, strength and sensitivity is cut off. He faces the danger of becoming useless and fruitless.

John 15:12-17

[12]"I demand that you love each other as much as I love you. [13]And here is how to measure it— the greatest love is shown when a person lays down his life for his friends; [14]And you are My friends if you obey Me. [15]I no longer call you slaves, for a master doesn't confide in his slaves; now you are My friends, proved by the fact that I have told you everything the Father told Me.

[16]"You didn't choose Me! I chose you! I appointed you to go and produce lovely fruit always, so that no matter what you ask for from the Father, using My name, He will give it to you.

[17]"I demand that you love each other . . .

How do you "lay down your life"?

Jesus seems to "switch gears" at this point. He has been talking about abiding in Him and vines and branches and suddenly He repeats his commandment that He had given earlier*—to love one another. Jesus says there is no greater love than to "lay down your life for a friend." What does this have to do with abiding in Christ and bearing fruit? Since one of the fruits of the Spirit—the primary

*John 13:34,35.

161

fruit of the Spirit in fact—is love, it evidently has a great deal to do with it.

But just how do you "lay down your life?" To do this literally is rather terminal. Furthermore, you don't really get too many opportunities to play hero and die for others. Is it possible for the typical Christian to "lay down his life for others" as he lives out the every-day nitty-gritty routine?

Felipe Alou, major league baseball star who has been a standout performer for the Giants as well as other teams, can say that he has personally experienced the kind of love that is willing to "lay down its life" for another. Felipe Alou is a Christian today because he had a friend named Roque Martinez. He and Roque went to school together in the Dominican Republic. Later Roque got a job in Canada and while working there, he became a Christian. Roque then returned to the Dominican Republic and enthusiastically shared his new faith with Felipe who was a bit embarrassed by Roque's religious fervor. These friends parted again in 1956 when Felipe went to Florida to play in the state league there. Before he left, Roque gave him a copy of a Spanish Bible and Felipe casually promised that he would read it.

For the next two years, Felipe Alou had one ambition—to reach the top, the major leagues. Every winter he would go home to the Dominican Republic and see his friend Roque again, and each time Roque would tell him, "I have been praying for you."

Felipe listened politely, but he didn't want to hurt his friend. He didn't want to tell Roque that while he was a Christian, he barely made a living as a concrete worker in the Dominican Republic; on the other hand, Felipe was living like a king as a minor league ball player—and he was doing it without Christ. Finally, in June of 1958 Felipe's big break came. The Giants notified him that they were bringing him out from their Seattle farm club and that he would be flown down to San Francisco the very next day to play his first major league game.

At almost the same time, a telegram arrived. It was from his friend Roque from faraway in the Dominican Republic. The telegram read: "Congratulations. Happy for you. One of my prayers has been answered. Am still praying that you will believe. Remember, even a big league ball-player needs Christ. You'll find that baseball is not everything. 'Be not wise in thine own eyes: fear the Lord and depart from evil' (Proverbs 3:7)."

Felipe was deeply moved—not so much by the Bible verse as he was by realizing how much it had cost his friend (who barely made enough to live on) to send an expensive telegram three thousand miles to tell him that he was praying for him.

Felipe flew down to San Francisco, but the game was rained out and he spent most of the rainy day in his hotel room staring at the telegram. "Then, at last," recalls Felipe Alou, "I got down on my knees and gave myself to the Lord. The next day, June 8, 1958, I played my first game as a major leaguer—and as a Christian."

Roque's prayer had been answered. In his own way, on his meager cement worker's salary in the Dominican Republic, Roque Martinez had "laid down a little bit of his life" for a friend and his friend had come to Christ.*

John 15:18-27

¹⁸"For you get enough hate from the world! But then, it hated Me before it hated you. ¹⁹The world would love you if you belonged to it; but you don't—for I chose you to come out of the world, and so it hates you. ²⁰Do you remember what I told you? 'A slave isn't greater than his master!' So since they persecuted Me, naturally they will persecute you. And if they had listened to Me, they would listen to you! ²¹The people of the world will persecute you because you belong to Me, for they don't know God who sent Me. ²²They would not be guilty if I had not come and spoken to them. But now they have no excuse for their sin. ²³Anyone hating Me is also hating My Father. ²⁴If I hadn't done such mighty miracles among them, they would not be counted guilty. But as it is, they saw these miracles and yet they hated both of us—Me and My Father. ²⁵This has fulfilled what the prophets said concerning the Messiah,

'They hated Me without reason.'

²⁶But I will send you the Comforter—the Holy Spirit, the source of all truth. He will come to you from the Father, and will tell you all about Me. ²⁷And you also must tell everyone about Me, because you have been with Me from the beginning."

"Abide"—that is, "let it happen"

These next statements by Jesus must have sounded awfully depressing to His disciples. The

---

*See Felipe Alou's personal testimony in *The Goal and the Glory*, edited by Ted Simonson, Fleming H. Revell Company, copyright 1962, p. 30. In another account of his conversion (*Play Ball!* by James C. Hefley, Zondervan Publications) Felipe Alou mentions the witness of Al Worthington, who was a pitcher with the Giants at that time. Worthington helped Felipe find real assurance that he knew Christ and belonged to Him.

world was to hate them because they would stand for what Jesus had taught. Before Jesus had come, the world had an excuse for its sin, but now that excuse was gone. Humanly speaking, being a disciple of Jesus didn't seem to have much future.

Except for one thing, and that one thing is mentioned in vs. 26 and 27. The "comforter" was to come—the Spirit of truth who would come from the Father and bear witness to Christ. And the disciples would be Christ's witnesses because they had been with Him.

Once again Jesus is emphasizing that without Him His disciples can do nothing. Unless they "abide in Him"; unless they trust Him and want to share their lives with Him, they cannot experience the Spirit of truth, whom He will send.

Is this still true for Christians today? And just exactly how can a Christian take practical steps to "abide in Christ" and to share his life with his Lord daily?

Because the word "abide" automatically suggests spending of time, it follows that the Christian has to come to terms with what has grown to be something of a bugaboo for many people—personal daily devotions, or as some call it, the "quiet time." Many Christians know the frustration that comes from trying to be "ruthlessly disciplined" to get up at 5:00 in the morning and read their portion of Scripture for the day. Many Christians know the dry dullness of slavishly going through the routine of turning pages of the Bible and repeating petitions from prayer lists that have very little personal meaning.

Still, there is no question that a quiet time with God is definitely a key part of learning to abide in Christ.

Is there a way to break out of the "devotional vitamin 'A' complex" that seems to make God into some sort of giant one-a-day capsule? Consider the following ideas offered by someone who grew up in a Christian home—as the daughter of a missionary, in fact—and who knows from personal experience that there is no automatic way to abide in Christ because when God made us new creations* He didn't make us automatons, He made us new people.

Make your time with God a "happening"

If you are feeling the "blahs" in your spiritual life; if you find yourself staring vacantly at your untouched Bible or Sunday School lesson; if your prayers to God seem as though they're flopping right back to earth like a burned out rocket, then maybe it's time for you to take spiritual inventory. Maybe you were once loaded with zeal for reading your Bible, praying and daily discovering Jesus Christ. But gradually the whole thing has become a burden or a cold routine, and you have to admit to yourself that either the Christian life *is* a stale proposition or *you have allowed* stagnation to set in.

Here are a few suggestions that may help vitalize your whole relationship with God.

1. *Choose a meaningful time to spend with God.* Talking with God is like going to the phone and calling up a terrific friend. You do it when you really feel in the mood. With God, of course, the lines are never busy. They are open and just waiting for you to make contact. Get used to talking with Him anytime you feel like it—in the locker room, in class (and not just before a test), in the halls, anywhere.

2. *Share your whole life's activities with God.* Naturally, you go to your best friend to talk for many reasons, not just

*II Cor. 5:17

when you are in a state of panic. The same is true with God. He is terribly interested in all parts of your life. Let Him in on your fears, disappointments, excitements and thrills. Never think anything is too small for His concern. If you have a personal relationship with Christ, treat Him like the real person that He is and not a vague idea.

3. *Use your common sense.* Assuming you have found some time alone and have opened your Bible or study guide, don't allow yourself to skim a few verses and then close it up with the sloppy excuse that it was too hard to understand. Nor should you finish reading and not know what you've just read. This is where you cheat God. Don't expect Him to make the words real to you when it is a matter of vocabulary. Use the dictionary! You would be surprised at its enlightenment. In addition to looking up the meaning of difficult words, a simple job of concentration on what you are reading will open up worlds of understanding.

4. *Tune in your imagination.* Before trying to apply a section of Scripture to yourself and your day, visualize the people and events of that day. Figure out the situations and problems. Ask yourself key questions using such words as who, what, where, when, how and why. As with any piece of literature, ask yourself what is the main idea of a chapter or book. Then look for different ways of applying it to yourself, trying to find broad principles.

5. *Turn on your intellect.* Don't sell yourself short on the question of how many verses should be read. No teacher in school would assign you just one or two paragraphs from a book for a day's assignment. Read large sections at a time. See how much more meaningful it is to read even an entire book of the Bible in one sitting. It is even a good idea for you to keep a notebook and make summaries of books or write outlines using the who, what, where words.

6. *Get helps.* Much of the thrill of Bible study is discovering for yourself what is there for you. In addition to a dictionary, use maps of Bible lands and times to locate the places mentioned. Use other translations besides the one you ordinarily read.

A good Bible commentary can also help (as long as you don't let it do all of your thinking for you). The best way to use a Bible commentary is to study the passage carefully for yourself and go as far with understanding the text as you can by using dictionaries and other references. Then, to get further light concerning particularly difficult words or ideas, check what the commentators have to say. Actually, it is best to have access to at least two commentaries in order to get comparative points of view.

Whatever way you choose to do your Bible study and talking to God, keep focused on the main purpose: which is to abide in (stay close to) Jesus Christ in a real and living relationship.*

TAKE TIME . . .

Without Me—nothing. The "vine and the branches" is one of the best known analogies in Scripture. Are you sure you have all the parts of the analogy straight? Who is the vine? Who is the "husbandman" or vinekeeper? Who are the branches? Why are the branches pruned?

Useless or useful? Read John 15:6-8. It's easy to take a verse like John 15:6 and get into the age old argument about the possibility of losing your salvation. But is that really the basic topic of John 15? Look carefully at vs. 7 and 8.

Live within my love. Read John 15:9-14. According to v. 13, what is the "greatest" kind of love? How do you interpret "laying down your life for your friends?" Would this necessarily mean dying for them in one noble courageous act? Or, are there other ways to "lay down your life" for your friends?

I chose you! Read John 15:15-17. According to these verses, what is the difference between a slave and a friend? How does Christ prove to you that He is your friend?

Enough hate from the world. Read John 15:18-25. Why does the world hate Christ? Why does the world hate the Christian? How do you feel about this? Is it worth it to be hated for Christ's sake? Why?

*"Make Your Time with God a Happening" is an article by free-lance writer, Marlene Hess. Mrs. Hess, daughter of Missionary parents, spent most of her childhood in Liberia. Returning to the United States during her teens, she attended high school at Wheaton Academy, Wheaton, Illinois; the Baptist Bible Seminary in Johnson City, New York for three years and was graduated from Wheaton College in 1964. Now the wife of lawyer Daniel Hess, Mrs. Hess teaches high school English in Grand Rapids, Michigan.

The source of all truth. Compare John 15:26-27 with Galatians 5:16-25. What kind of fruit has Christ actually been talking about in this 15th chapter? According to Galatians 5, why is it difficult to bear fruit?

TAKE ACTION . . .

Pick one area of your life and take specific steps to share it more freely with your Lord this week.

Try "laying down your life" for one of your friends this week. That is, try really going out of your way for one of your friends and putting yourself out for him. What ever you do for this friend, do it with utterly no desire to be "paid back." Perhaps your friend won't even notice it; but you will.

Try using some of Marlene Hess' ideas (see pp. 165-168) to take the "blahs" out of your spiritual life.

TAKE INVENTORY . . .

Take a few moments to sit quietly and think through exactly who is in charge in your life. Are you "abiding in Christ"—that is, are you really sharing your life with Him and letting Him share His life with you? Or are you "dropping in occasionally"?

In what way have you "laid down your life" for your friends, loved ones, family, others? That is, what have you done lately to "put yourself out," to sacrifice yourself or your interests in some way for the good of another?

Take inventory on your quiet time. The first question concerns whether there is any quiet time on which to take inventory. It is all well and good to say that you can be in touch with Jesus anytime, anywhere and that you know you can pray anytime in any position. But this is sort of like saying that you could carry on an intimate conversation with a good friend in a boiler factory. If you really love someone and enjoy his company—if you really want to abide with him and share your life with him—you seek out situations and ways to spend time with this person and to get to know him better.

CHAPTER 14

Do Christians have what it takes?

Do I have what it takes?

We all ask ourselves this question in one way or another every day. We wonder if we have what it takes to pass the test, finish the course, complete the job on time, sell the desired quota, convince a certain person of our position, deliver the goods on the athletic field. The list can go on and on. Life is a series of situations that keep haunting us with the question: "Do you have what it takes to do *this*?"

What about witnessing? What about communicating Christ, telling it like it is about your experience with Him? Any Christian might well wonder if he "has what it takes" to witness effectively today.

As perhaps in no other time in history, the Christian finds it hard to present the Gospel because of two overwhelming attitudes. One of these is the attitude of *subjectivism*. People today are the "enlightened recipients" of a great deal of education. Secular educators drum one thing into their students from the cradle on: all truth is relative and you can't know anything for sure. Today people have the decided idea that their opinion on something is just as good as another person's.

The other attitude is one of *scientism*. There are many today who prefer the rationalistic, humanistic approach to life. The idea of "God" is for small children or the feeble-minded. The healthy well-adjusted 20th century man doesn't need God. He can solve his own problems and get his own answers to the questions that face him.

With hearts fast becoming as transplantable as geraniums, with the moon only a few more space shots away, with cancer almost conquered, with science making more progress in the 20th century than was experienced in all of the known preceding time of man on this earth, it is not hard to understand why some people feel that their god is science and their great high priest is the computer.

And so, the Christian trembles a bit as he looks around himself—at a secular society where his views about Christ and God are considered everything from quaint to kooky. It is not hard to understand why he might wonder if he has what it takes to win people to Christ.

Christians often take one of two approaches to the question of having what it takes to witness. Some of them go at it tooth and nail with sheer force of personality, with militant zeal, as knights charging

171

into battle. After all, is the world not the enemy? Shouldn't Satan be dealt mortal blows at every opportunity?

Some of these people are very successful. They obtain from their victims decisions of various kinds. Or at least they succeed in scoring many direct hits with Biblical bullets and Gospel napalm. These witnesses are often heard to say that they are praising the Lord because they have now converted their 89th or 122nd (or whatever figure it might be) person to the Lord.

A far more common attitude to the question of having what it takes, however, is one of discouragement. The proud fireballs who seem so successful at witnessing don't help matters any for the discouraged Christians who decide that they don't have what it takes. They can't talk fast or very cleverly. At just the crucial moment they forget all the Bible verses that they have memorized. Furthermore, they are (frankly) a little bit afraid to bring up the subject of Christ and religion with unbelievers.

Both of these attitudes—the attitude of zealous pride and the attitude of discouragement completely miss the mark. Both are wrong because both fail to take into account the Lord's promise in chapter 16 of John. Both of the attitudes are in error because they fail to recognize that witnessing is always at least a "two-person" proposition. The Christian, you see, never witnesses alone. . . .

John 16:1-15

[1]"I have told you these things so that you won't be staggered by all that lies ahead." [2]"For you will be ex-

communicated from the synagogues, and indeed the time is coming when those who kill you will think they are doing God a service. ³This is because they have never known the Father or Me. ⁴Yes, I'm telling you these things now so that when they happen you will remember I warned you. I didn't tell you earlier because I was going to be with you for a while longer. ⁵But now I am going away to the one who sent Me; and none of you seems interested in the purpose of My going; none wonders why.ᵛ ⁶Instead you are only filled with sorrow. ⁷But the fact of the matter is that it is best for you that I go away, for if I don't, the Comforter won't come. If I do, He will—for I will send Him to you. ⁸And when He has come He will convince the world of its sin, and of the availability of God's goodness, and of deliverance from judgment.ʷ ⁹The world's sin is unbelief in Me; ¹⁰There is righteousness available because I go to the Father and you shall see Me no more; ¹¹There is deliverance from judgment because the prince of this world has already been judged.

¹²"Oh, there is so much more I want to tell you, but you can't understand it now. ¹³When the Holy Spirit, who is truth, comes, He shall guide you into all truth, for He will not be presenting His own ideas, but will be passing on to you what He has heard. He will tell you about the future. ¹⁴He shall praise Me and bring Me great honor by showing you My glory. ¹⁵All the Father's glory is Mine; this is what I mean when I say that He will show you My glory."

How to take off the pressure

It must have been puzzling for the disciples to keep hearing Jesus say it would be better for them if He would go away. That just didn't seem to add up—especially after He had just told them that in order to be able to do anything they had to "abide in" or stay with Him. But what Jesus was telling His disciples was that during his earthly ministry, even though He was God Himself, He was still limited. For example, He could only be in one place at a time. But Christ's Gospel was not destined to be limited to a comfortable little clique of Galilean fishermen. Christ had bigger plans than that because Christ is God and God has a plan for the entire world. And that was what Jesus was telling His disciples. Christ the man would have to leave them, but He would send the Holy Spirit, Who could be everywhere at once, working God's will according to God's perfect plan.

But why does Jesus keep calling the Holy Spirit the Comforter or the Counsellor? Did Jesus mean that there would be some sort of "representative of God" who would come; some sort of "John the Baptist come lately" who would arrive on the scene after Jesus was gone, to dry the eyes of the weeping disciples?

The Greek word used here is "paraclete," which means "one who stands beside." Some translators use the word Counsellor instead of Comforter because they believe the idea of a counsellor better conveys the thought that Jesus was trying to communicate. Today people get different images, when they hear the word "counsellor." The high school or college student thinks of the person who helps him choose courses of study, gives him advice on problems and helps him make plans for the future. Those who have anything to do with the courts of law think of a lawyer, a man who "counsels" his client and defends him in court. And there are also marriage counsellors, camp counsellors, psychological counsellors, etc. A counsellor is one who is there to help, to point certain things out, to convince his client of a certain truth.

In John 16:8 Christ points out that the Holy Spirit will do counselling among unbelievers as well as Christians. The Holy Spirit will convict or convince the world of sin, righteousness and judgment. As the *Living New Testament* paraphrase puts it so well, "He will convince the world of its sin, and of the availability of God's goodness, and of deliverance from judgment."

The task of "convincing the world of sin" is a crucial one. Unless a man has a sense of sin, he cannot sense the need of a Saviour. Unless a person realizes he is guilty, he cannot desire a pardon. Unless a person realizes he is lost, he cannot be interested in being saved. It is the Holy Spirit that convinces people that they are sinners. The Spirit convicts or convinces them of their own guilt. The Spirit does this by showing people how they measure up against the goodness and righteousness of God.

This is an obvious truth that Christians sometimes overlook. It is quite easy for the Christian to fall into the trap of thinking that he has to convict or convince a person of his sinfulness. Some Christians become very skillful in "Bible bushwhacking." They shoot down their victims with a fusillade of carefully memorized Scripture missiles. When the victim finally stomps off in anger, the Bible bushwhacker thinks: "Well, I guess I really convicted him that time!" But, this kind of anger is not necessarily due to conviction caused by the Holy Spirit. On the contrary, this kind of anger can make a person deaf to anything the Spirit might have to say.

Actually, it is not the Christian's job to convince or convict anyone of anything, as John 16:7,8 point out. The Christian is to witness and to communicate his own personal experience with Christ. The Holy Spirit will do the convicting or convincing of the unbeliever and show him his sin in comparison to God's righteousness. Once the Christian truly grasps the significance of this teaching in John 16:8, a great deal of the pressure goes out of witnessing. The burden of bringing the conviction isn't on the Christian; it's where it belongs—on the Holy Spirit Himself.

Can you think of any situations where the pressure has been off of you and on someone else? For example, you are driving with a friend and he is stopped for speeding. There is no pressure on you; you can sit there and listen to the officer lecture your friend and (hopefully) give him a "warning" ticket. But suppose you had switched places with your friend before the officer came up to the car because your friend had no driver's license and you did. Would there be pressure then? Your stomach would feel like a butterfly convention.

There are countless illustrations. Athletes know what it's like to have a "monkey on their back"—to have the fate of the game in their hands as they step to the free-throw line, step to the plate with the bases loaded in the last of the ninth, or get ready to kick that all-important point after touchdown. Although many of them may not want to admit it, they're glad when these plays have to be made by a teammate and not by themselves.

The point is that the job of convicting someone and actually changing his mind and his heart is not the Christian's. This is the work of the Holy Spirit. When the Christian tends to his end of the job—and allows the Holy Spirit to do His work of convicting and convincing, the Christian can relax, or at least he can feel more at ease. But if the Christian tries to step in and do the task that is not his responsibility and for which he is not equipped, for which he has no power, he will botch up the entire operation. He will "blow the whole ball game." To put it another way, when the Christian tries to go it on his own he cuts himself off from his own source of power.

Still fresh in the memory of many is the huge power failure that involved much of the northeast United States in November, 1965. At 5:18 p.m., New York City went black, as well as the entire state. The area affected covered some 80,000 square miles and took in part of seven U.S. states and most of Canada's province of Ontario. Whether it was a generator feeding power at the wrong frequency or a switch thrown in error by some utility company employee, was hard to determine.

But the millions of people living in New York and the surrounding area quickly determined that the lights were out, the power was off, and many of them were stuck for the night in subway train stations, office buildings, in tunnels under the East River, etc.

The blackout left some 200 planes in the air above New York's Kennedy International airport.

All of these aircraft had to be rerouted to air fields in other states where runway lights were still burning. Overall loss in business due to the blackout, which lasted in some areas up to 13 hours, was estimated at $100,000,000. A tire company, for example, lost $50,000 worth of tires when power failed during a critical curing process. A car manufacturer had to throw away 50 engine blocks because high speed drills froze while boring piston holes. Bakeries in New York alone reported a loss of 300,000 loaves of bread, which were spoiled when the power went off.

All in all, modern civilization as Americans and Canadians knew it that November night came to a halt because the power supply on which they were depended had been cut off.*

The Christian, too, has a power supply on which he is completely dependent. As John 16:8-15 points out, the Holy Spirit is the supply. The Holy Spirit not only does the job of convicting and convincing the world of sin and God's righteousness and God's judgment; the Holy Spirit guides the Christian into all truth. But when the Christian "cuts off the current" by quenching the Holy Spirit, his productive activity ceases. Just as New Yorkers groped around in darkened subways and tunnels under the East River on the night of the biggest blackout they ever experienced, the Christian who dims the power of the Holy Spirit in his life walks about in spiritual weakness. But unlike the victims of the

*For a complete report on the 1965 power failure in the Northeastern United States, see "The Biggest Blackout," *Time*, November 19, 1965, p. 36.

1965 power failure, the Christian need not wait for hours for the power to go back on. He can turn the power back on any time he chooses. He only has to throw the switches marked "faith" and "obedience" and the spiritual lights will go on again.

John 16:16-33

¹⁶"In just a little while I will be gone, and you will see Me no more; but just a little while after that, and you will see Me again!"

¹⁷,¹⁸"Whatever is He saying?" some of His disciples asked. "What is this about 'going to the Father'? We don't know what He means!"

¹⁹Jesus realized they wanted to ask Him so He said, "Are you asking yourselves what I mean? ²⁰The world will greatly rejoice over what is going to happen to Me, and you will weep. But your weeping shall suddenly be turned to wonderful joy [when you see Me again]. ²¹It will be the same joy as that of a woman in labor when her child is born—her anguish gives place to rapturous joy and the pain is forgotten. ²²You have sorrow now, but I will see you again and then you will rejoice; and no one can rob you of that joy. ²³At that time you won't need to ask Me for anything, for you can go directly to the Father and ask Him, and He will give you what you ask for because you use My name. ²⁴You haven't tried this before, [but begin now*]. Ask, using My name, and you will receive, and your cup of joy will overflow."

²⁵"I have spoken of these matters very guardedly, but the time will come when this will not be necessary and I will tell you plainly all about the Father. ²⁶Then you will present your petitions over My signature!ʸ And I won't need to ask the Father to grant you these requests, ²⁷for the Father Himself loves you dearly because you love Me and believe that I came from the Father. ²⁸Yes, I came from the Father into the world and will leave the world and return to the Father."

[29]"At last You are speaking plainly," His disciples said, "and not in riddles. [30]Now we understand that You know everything and don't need anyone to tell You anything.* From this we believe that You came from God."

[31]"Do you finally believe this?" Jesus asked. [32]"But the time is coming—in fact, it is here—when you will be scattered, each one returning to his own home, leaving Me alone. Yet I will not be alone, for the Father is with Me. [33]I have told you all this so that you will have peace of heart and mind. Here on earth you will have many trials and sorrows; but cheer up, for I have overcome the world."

The dependable Christian is dependent

There is an underlying message in the words of the final verses of John 16. It is the kind of message that is not acceptable in today's hard-hitting world where success is measured by how well one runs the rat race, how well one manipulates his income tax return, and how well one faces the world by standing on his own two feet and carving out his destiny with his own hands.

But actually, the Christian lives according to reversed values. In the words of Dick Halverson ... "Self-sufficiency is not a mark of greatness! The truly great man is acutely aware of his limitations! He is not overcome by them ... but he is aware of them! It is the little—pig-headed—rambunctious man that is self-sufficient—because he is unconscious of his limitations—insensitive to his dependence upon others or God. Being so impressed with himself, he is impervious to criticism or suggestions.

"Rather than admit dependence, the little man bluffs his way through ... and when he fails,

THE 'LITTLE' MAN IS 'SELF-SUFFICIENT'

blames circumstances or others (he never blames himself!)

"Convincing himself that someone else or something else is to blame—he loses one more opportunity to know himself—his limitations. Becoming more entrenched in his own self-delusion, he plows ahead in pseudo-self confidence.

"... The little man swells instead of growing, the big man is humble, not simply because it's right to be—but because of his sensitivity to his dependence upon others... and mostly upon God!

"The greatest man who ever lived was the most dependent man in history! 'I do nothing of myself,' said He.

"Jesus Christ was totally adequate for any situation—any task—any contingency ... because He was completely dependent upon His heavenly Father.

"The man who most relies on God will be most reliable!"*

And the way to rely on God is to listen to the Spirit, to walk after Him, to depend completely upon Him in all that you do.

Does the Christian have what it takes to communicate Christ? Yes, indeed. He has the Holy Spirit. The question for the Christian is not, "Do I have what it takes?" The question is, "Do I make use of what I have by trusting in Him—in the Holy Spirit of Christ, God Himself, living in me, available at all times and fully sufficient for everything that He wants me to do?"

John 17:1-26

[1]When Jesus had finished saying all these things He looked up to heaven and said, "Father, the time has come. Reveal the glory of Your Son so that He can give the glory back to You. [2]For You have given Him authority over every man and woman in all the earth. He gives eternal life to each one You have given Him. [3]And this is the way to have eternal life—by knowing You, the only true God, and Jesus Christ, the one You sent to earth!

[4]"I brought glory to You here on earth by doing everything You told Me to. [5]And now, Father, reveal My glory as I stand in Your presence, the glory We shared before the world began. [6]I have told these men all about You. They were in the world, but then You gave them to Me. Actually, they were always Yours, and You gave them to Me; and they have obeyed You. [7]Now they know that everything I have is a gift from

*Perspective, Richard Halverson, Volume 20, No. 17, April 24, 1968.

You, ⁸For I have passed on to them the commands You gave Me; and they accepted them and know of a certainty that I came down to earth from You, and they believe You sent Me.

⁹"My plea is not for the world but for these You have given Me because they belong to You. ¹⁰And all of them, since they are Mine, belong to You; and You have given them back to Me with everything else of Yours, and so *they are My glory!* ¹¹Now I am leaving the world, and leaving them behind, and coming to You. Holy Father, keep them in Your own care—all those You have given Me—so that they will be united just as We are, with none missing. ¹²During My time here I have kept safe within Your family* all of these You gave to Me. I guarded them so that not one perished, except the son of hell, as the Scriptures foretold.

¹³"And now I am coming to You. I have told them many things while I was with them so that they would be filled with My joy. ¹⁴I have given them Your commands. And the world hates them because they don't fit in with it, just as I don't. ¹⁵I'm not asking You to take them out of the world, but to keep them safe from Satan's power. ¹⁶They are not part of this world any more than I am. ¹⁷Make them pure and holy through teaching them Your words of truth. ¹⁸As You sent Me into the world, I am sending them into the world, ¹⁹and I consecrate Myself to meet their need for growth in truth and holiness.

²⁰"I am not praying for these alone but also for all future believers who will come to Me because of the testimony of these. ²¹My prayer for all of them is that they will be of one heart and mind, just as You and I are, Father—that just as You are in Me and I am in You, so they will be in Us. ²²I have given them the glory You gave Me—the glorious unity of being one, as We are—²³I in them and You in Me, all being perfected into one—so that the world will know You sent Me and will understand that You love them as much

183

as You love Me. ²⁴Father, I want them with Me—
these You've given Me—so that they can see My
glory. You gave Me the glory because You loved Me
before the world began! ²⁵O righteous Father, the
world doesn't know You, but I do; and these disciples
know You sent Me. ²⁶And I have revealed You to them,
and will keep on revealing You so that the mighty love
You have for Me may be in them, and I in them."

Jesus' prayer for you and me

Without question, John 17 is holy ground. Bible
scholars call it the "center of sanctity," the "holy of
holies." The reason they do is because John 17 is a
prayer—and even more important it is the conversation between Jesus and His Heavenly Father. It is
as if you were eavesdropping on a dialogue within
the Trinity. Here you are truly getting a firsthand
look at the mind of God.

In this passage, Jesus prayed for Himself (vs.
1-5).

He prayed for His disciples—the eleven who are
left with Him (vs. 6-19).

He prayed for Christian believers, the handful
that believed in Him that night, and also all those
who would believe in Him in the future (vs. 20-26).

As He prayed for His disciples, Jesus asked for
four things: that they would be preserved from the
power of the present world; that they would have
unity; that they would have joy; that they would be
sanctified (set apart for a holy purpose) by God
Himself. And, because Jesus said in v. 20 that He
did not pray for the disciples only but also for those
that believe in Him, He certainly made these same
requests for all believers for all time.

184

Unfortunately, the world sees a church today that seems to suggest that Christ's prayer has gone unanswered. While struggling desperately to keep out certain forms of "worldliness," the church has become isolated from the world it is trying to reach with the Gospel. Minister-writer Jess E. Moody puts it like this:

We may worship our exclusiveness so much as to be repudiated by the lost world outside. We cannot strut arrogantly and blindly in a smog of smugness. This always leads to Pharisaism.

God never told us to be dour judges, standing in the robes of prudery. We are in a business of redemptive involvement—not hyper-righteous investigation.

Modern Christians must realize that we are in sales—not management. The management of affairs of men belongs to God Himself.

The Father, Son and Holy Spirit are saying: 'Leave the driving to Us.'

We do have a fight on our hands, and we can win—because, as Ethel Waters once remarked, "Jesus don't sponsor no flops."

The battle lines must be drawn with institutionalized evil: with all the powers that despise the human spirit.

We cannot win if we pit a lukewarm Church against a burning paganism.

But even more condemning than its isolationism is the church's lack of unity. Jesus' prayer was that His followers would be of "one heart and mind, just as You and I are, Father—that just as You are in Me and I am in You, so they will be in Us" (v. 21).

But, sad to say, that is not "how it is" in all too many churches. What is the reason? Author Moody narrows it down to this:

A church that isn't evangelistic isn't a church.

A church that ceases to be evangelistic will cease to be evangelical and missionary.

There is no use taking a lamp to Malaysia that won't burn at home.

A church that ceases to be evangelistic will be a divided church.

Brethern, cease your feuding, and fish!

It is difficult to be interested in witnessing if all our energy is wasted in a deacon's meeting, which too often is a long hot ride through ulcer gulch.

More church feuds are solved by evangelism than this world dreams of.

You can't fish and fight at the same time. You must neglect your net or your gun.

There is one other thought from John 17 that is both a comfort and a challenge. In v. 14 Jesus observes that the world hates His followers because "they don't fit in with it, just as I don't." And then Jesus goes on to say, "I'm not asking You to take them out of the world, but to keep them safe from Satan's power." In these words, as perhaps in no other place in John, Jesus is giving his followers a commission to go out and "tell it like it is." Jess Moody has a few words on that idea too:

We must throw overboard the heresy that the church house is the best place to witness.

Remember, it is the Sermon on the Mount—not the sermon in the cathedral.

Let us pray until we are filled with the Holy Spirit.

Then we can fish anywhere and the nets will be overloaded and overtaxed.

Let us not fear collision with reality. That is the one place the Lord will be. Let us not seek uncritical acceptance, that is the one place the Lord will not be.

The carnal way to save our lives is to never risk them.

The spiritual way is to see the churning flood of human hatred, hurl ourselves into it, knowing that Christ promises that we will surface again after the wave is dead.*

*Quotations by Jess Moody from the book *A Drink at Joel's Place*, Jess Moody, Word Books, Waco, Texas.

TAKE TIME...

Do you know what you're in for? Read John 16:1-4. Christ warns His disciples that there will be persecution and possibly even death. Do you think most Christians really count the cost that is predicted here? What would happen in your church if persecution really came? What would happen in your own life?

A "selfish" kind of sorrow? Read John 16:5,6. As usual, Christ is very candid with His disciples as well as very kind. He tells them that they are grieved with the prospect of His departure because they are afraid for themselves, but none of them seem to want to know just why He is going. In other words, they are approaching the situation from a very natural and self-centered standpoint. But they are not concerned about the greater plan of God. Is this still happening among Christians today? Why does it happen? Why does it happen in your life?

When I go He will come. Read John 16:7 and compare with John 14:16, 26; John 15:26. This is Jesus' fourth mention of the Holy Spirit. Note how He tells a little more about the Spirit each time He mentions Him. Why would the coming of the Holy Spirit be best for the disciples? What does the departure of Jesus and the coming of the Holy Spirit have to do with you?

The Holy Spirit's work in the world. Read John 16:8-11, especially in the *Living New Testament* paraphrase on page 173. Notice how v. 8 clearly sums up the work of the Holy Spirit. If the work of the Holy Spirit is convincing the world of its sin and of God's righteousness and judgment, what is the work of the Christian?

The Holy Spirit's work in the Christian. Read John 16:12-15. Note especially v. 13. The Spirit will guide the Christian into all truth, but He will not speak on only His own authority. What does this tell you about the Trinity and the mind of God?

Eavesdropping on God. Read John 17:1-19. John 17 is considered one of the most profound passages in all Scripture. It is Christ's intercessory (high priestly) prayer for His followers and all those who believe in Him. In these first 19 verses, Christ prays for Himself and His disciples. Read these verses carefully and pick out the most significant request that Jesus makes for His disciples. See especially vs. 13-19.

Of one heart and mind? Read John 17:20-26. In these verses, Jesus prays for all future believers who will become Christians because of the disciples' testimony. Do you think His request in v. 21 has been answered? Why? Why not? What keeps this request by Christ from being answered? What keeps it from being answered in your life?

TAKE INVENTORY . . .

Analyze the way you go about witnessing. Are you trying to do more of the work than is necessary? Do you often feel that you have to "argue" or "defend your position"? Have you been fully aware that the Holy Spirit is "witnessing with you" and that it is up to Him to do the convicting and converting while it is up to you to "tell it like it is"?

Analyze the times in your life when you experienced spiritual power failure. Why does this happen? See if you can trace it back to one of these causes: forgetting about God and the Holy Spirit within you; putting yourself ahead of God; being too proud to rely on the Holy Spirit and trying to "do the driving yourself."

TAKE ACTION . . .

Pray for the Holy Spirit to lead you to someone with whom you can share Christ. Witness to this person with full awareness that the Holy Spirit is by your side doing any convicting and converting that is necessary. See if this new approach doesn't take a lot of the pressure out of witnessing for Christ?

If you have been part of any feuds, disagreements, or "cold wars" in your church or Christian group, see what you can do to remedy the situation with positive plans and action to reach out to win others instead of continuing to be ingrown and divided. In the words of Jess Moody, "You can't fight and fish at the same time."

CHAPTER 15

The most
important event in history

If you were asked, "What do you believe is the most important event of all history?" how would you answer?

The evolutionist would probably look back to the day when a certain primate came down out of the trees and started to walk erect.

The philosopher might look back to the day that Socrates was born or perhaps he would prefer Plato.

The student of American history might choose October 12, 1492—the day that Columbus "discovered America." Or perhaps he would prefer July 4th, 1776 (although there might be Britishers who would not agree).

There might be many living in this century who prefer more recent dates: the armistice for World War I, November 11, 1918; V-E Day, May 8, 1945; or V-J Day, August 14, 1945.

Those who are scientifically oriented might think

of October 4, 1957 with the hurling of the first satellite into space by the Russians, Sputnik I. Those who are medically oriented might consider the date of the first heart transplant, December 3, 1967.

But for the Christian, there is one event that towers above all others—as high as the heavens are above the earth—and that is the event that changed the course of all history and the destiny of all mankind: the crucifixion and resurrection of Jesus Christ. All other dates, you see, involve the works and experiences of men. But the crucifixion and the resurrection tell us of the works of God among men. It didn't seem that way the day that they dragged the political prisoner before Pilate. In fact, when this Galilean rabble-rouser talked about truth, Pilate sneered in His face and asked Him, "What is truth?" What Pilate didn't seem to know that day was that he was as close as a man could get to truth and still not know it for himself. . .

John 18:1-40

¹After saying these things Jesus crossed the Kidron ravine with His disciples and entered a grove of olive trees. ²Judas, the betrayer, knew this place, for Jesus had gone there many times with His disciples. ³The chief priests and Pharisees had given Judas a squad of soldiers and police to accompany him. Now with blazing torches, lanterns, and weapons they arrived at the olive grove. ⁴Jesus fully realized all that was going to happen to Him. Stepping forward to meet them He asked, "Whom are you looking for?"

⁵"Jesus of Nazareth," they replied.

"I am He," Jesus said.

⁶And as He said it, they all fell backwards to the

ground! 'Once more He asked them, "Who are you searching for?"

And again they replied, "Jesus of Nazareth."

⁸"I told you I am He," Jesus said; "and since I am the one you are after, let these others go." ⁹He did this to carry out the prophecy He had just made, "I have not lost a single one of those You gave Me . . ."

¹⁰Then Simon Peter drew a sword and slashed off the right ear of Malchus, the High Priest's servant. ¹¹But Jesus said to Peter, "Put your sword away. Shall I not drink from the cup the Father has given Me?"

¹²So the Jewish police with the soldiers and their lieutenant arrested Jesus and tied Him. ¹³First they took Him to Annas, the father-in-law of Caiaphas, the High Priest that year. ¹⁴Caiaphas was the one who told the other Jewish leaders, "Better that one should die for all." ¹⁵Simon Peter followed along behind, as did another of the disciples who was acquainted with the High Priest. So that other disciple was permitted into the courtyard along with Jesus, ¹⁶while Peter stood outside the gate. Then the other disciple spoke to the girl watching at the gate, and she let Peter in. ¹⁷The girl asked Peter, "Aren't you one of Jesus' disciples?"

"No," he said, "I am not!"

¹⁸The police and the household servants were standing around a fire they had made, for it was cold. And Peter stood there with them, warming himself.

¹⁹Inside, the High Priest began asking Jesus about His followers and what He had been teaching them.

²⁰Jesus replied, "What I teach is widely known, for I have preached regularly in the synagogue and Temple; I have been heard by all the Jewish leaders and teach nothing in private that I have not said in public. ²¹Why are you asking Me this question? Ask those who heard Me. You have some of them here. They know what I said."

²²One of the soldiers standing there struck Jesus with his fist. "Is that the way to answer the High Priest?" he demanded.

[23]"If I lied, prove it," Jesus said. "Should you hit a man for telling the truth?"

[24]Then Annas sent Jesus, bound, to Caiaphas the High Priest.

[25]Meanwhile, as Simon Peter was standing by the fire, he was asked again, "Aren't you one of His disciples?"

"Of course not," he replied.

[26]But one of the household slaves of the High Priest —a relative of the man whose ear Peter had cut off— asked, "Didn't I see you out there in the olive grove with Jesus?"

[27]Again Peter denied it. And immediately a rooster crowed.

[28]Jesus' trial before Caiaphas ended in the early hours of the morning. Next He was taken to the palace of the Roman governor.[b] His accusers wouldn't go in themselves for that would "defile"[c] them, they said, and they wouldn't be allowed to eat the Passover lamb. [29]So Pilate, the governor, went out to them and asked, "What is your charge against this man? What are you accusing him of doing?"

[30]"We wouldn't have arrested him if he weren't a criminal!" they retorted.

[31]"Then take him away and judge him yourselves by your own laws," Pilate told them.

"But we want him crucified," they said, "and your approval is required."[d] [32]This fulfilled Jesus' prediction concerning the method of His execution.[e]

[33]Then Pilate went back into the palace and called for Jesus to be brought to him, "Are you the King of the Jews?" he asked Him.

[34]"'King' as *you* use the word or as the *Jews* use it?" Jesus asked.[f]

[35]"Am I a Jew?" Pilate retorted. "Your own people and their chief priests brought you here. Why? What have you done?"

[36]Then Jesus answered, "I am not an earthly king. If I were, My followers would have fought when I

was arrested by the Jewish leaders. But My Kingdom is not of the world."

[37]Pilate replied, "But you are a king then?"

"Yes," Jesus said. "I was born for that purpose. And I came to bring truth to the world. All who love the truth are My followers."

[38]"What is truth?" Pilate exclaimed. Then he went out again to the people and told them, "He is not guilty of any crime. [39]But you have a custom of asking me to release someone from prison each year at Passover. So if you want me to, I'll release the 'King of the Jews.'"

[40]But they screamed back, "No! Not this man but Barabbas!" Barabbas was a robber.

Yes, just what is "truth"?

Things move fast in this chapter. There is the arrest in the Garden as Judas makes good his plan of betrayal. There is the mockery of a trial that must have made Lady Justice blush through her blindfold. There is Peter's denial, precisely as his Lord had predicted, but instead of saying to Peter "Well, He told you so" we can only wonder what we would have done. And then there is the scene before Pilate, and here we find the Lord Jesus Christ still "telling it like it is"—not giving any impassioned defense for Himself, but simply witnessing quietly before men who are cynical, skeptical, and unbelieving. "I came to bring truth to the world," Jesus told Pilate. "All who love the truth are My followers" (John 18:37—*Living New Testament*).

And Pilate looked back and asked a question that doesn't ring with irony; it just seems to hit with a dull thud: "What is truth?"

Did Pilate know who Jesus was? Whether he did or not, it is obvious he didn't "know" Jesus. He didn't know Him as the Son of God and as his Saviour. It is all like some sort of tragi-comedy. God Himself being judged by a man who cynically asks, "What is truth?" Pilate was looking truth in the eye, and didn't know it.

The same thing has been going on ever since. People constantly are confronted by Christ, who is the Way, the Truth, and the Life. They hear Christ's amazing claims, but their only question in return is, "What is truth?"

But many have responded differently. Many have finally seen that their search for truth has ended.

For example, internationally known surgeon Dr. Howard A. Kelly of John Hopkins University wrestled with the question, "What is truth?" Dr. Kelly's problem centered on whether he could trust the Bible. Critics of Scripture who "tore the Bible apart" with their own humanistic interpretations and theories left Dr. Kelly floundering. But as he recalls, "In one thing the higher critics, like the modernists, overreached themselves: in claiming that the Gospel of John was not written in John's time but well after the first century, perhaps as late as 150 A.D. Now, if any part of the Bible is assuredly the very Word of God speaking through His servant, it is John's Gospel. To ask me to believe that so inexpressibly marvelous a book was written long after all the events by some admiring follower, and was not inspired directly by the Spirit of God, is asking me to accept a miracle far greater than any of those recorded in the Bible."

PEOPLE HAVE DIFFERENT ANSWERS FOR THE
QUESTION: 'WHAT IS TRUTH?'

In truly scientific tradition, Dr. Kelly decided to
test the Bible, to try it to see if it would really work.
And so he did. He took the Bible as the authorita-
tive textbook of the Christian faith just as he would
accept a treatise on any earthly science. He submitted to its conditions according to Christ's invitation
and promise that, "If any man will do his will, he
shall know the doctrine, whether it be of God, or
whether I speak of myself" (John 7:17).

Dr. Kelly writes that the outcome has been his
acceptance of the Bible as the Word of God and his
acceptance of the Lord Jesus Christ as the only
begotten Son of God and Saviour of the world.

He writes: "Again, as faith reveals God my
Father and Christ my Saviour, I follow without
question where He leads me daily by His Spirit of
love, wisdom, power and prayer. I place His precepts and His leadings above every seeming proba-

bility, dismissing cherished convictions and holding the wisdom of man as folly when opposed to Him."*

What is truth? Bernie Allen, all-round athlete who made the big leagues with the Minnesota Twins, recalls an experience in college when he was glad that he knew the truth in Christ. In 1960, he was quarterback for the Purdue University Boilermakers. On the way home from a game with Minnesota, the two-engine DC-3 in which the Purdue team was riding developed engine trouble. One of the engines died and the other one nearly caught fire. As Allen puts it, "At a time like that, you find out whether or not you are afraid to die and whether or not you really love the Lord."

Allen recalls that a lot of players were scared and many were praying. Allen prayed, too, but he wasn't really frightened. "I knew that if it was my time to go, I was ready, for I knew the Lord. I have no doubt that at any time He is ready to take me, I am ready; for that is where I want to go—to heaven." Allen also remembers that he had the opportunity to share the truth that kept him calm with some of his teammates.**

Bernie Allen's faith in the Truth—Jesus Christ— gave him peace of mind that day when he rode a two engine plane that came in on half a motor. It seems that knowing the Truth and having peace of mind often go together. But Pilate had no peace of mind that day when Jesus stood before him. He turned to the crowd and said that he could find no

*Quotes by Dr. Kelly taken from his testimony in "Out of Doubt, into Faith," American Tract Society, Oradell, N. J.
**See "Safe at Home," *Decision*, May, 1963, p. 7.

crime that Jesus had done. According to Jewish custom, one man was to be released from prison each year at Passover time. Pilate gave the crowd a choice: he would release Jesus or Barabbas (a local bandit of some repute). Pilate was sure they would pick Jesus, but they didn't. Now there was nothing for Pilate to do but to go through with it...

John 19:1-42

¹Then Pilate laid open Jesus' back with a leaded whip, ²And the soldiers made a crown of thorns and placed it on His head and robed Him in royal* purple. ³"Hail, 'King of the Jews!'" they mocked and struck Him with their fists.

⁴Pilate went outside again and said to the Jews, "I am going to bring him out to you now, but understand clearly that I find him NOT GUILTY."

⁵Then Jesus came out wearing the crown of thorns and the purple robe. And Pilate said, "Behold the man!"

⁶At sight of Him the chief priests and Jewish officials began yelling, "Crucify! Crucify!"

"*You* crucify him," Pilate said. "I find him NOT GUILTY."

⁷They replied, "By our laws he ought to die because he called himself the Son of God."

⁸When Pilate heard this, he was more frightened than ever. ⁹He took Jesus back into the palace again and asked Him, "Where are you from?" But Jesus gave no answer.

¹⁰"You won't talk to me?" Pilate demanded. "Don't you realize that I have the power to release you or to crucify you?"

¹¹Then Jesus said, "You would have no power at all over Me unless it were given to you from above. So those^h who brought Me to you have the greater sin."

¹²Then Pilate tried to release Him, but the Jewish leaders told him, "If you release this man, you are no

friend of Caesar's. Anyone who declares himself a king is a rebel against Caesar."

[13]At these words Pilate brought Jesus out to them again and sat down at the judgment bench on the stone-paved platform.[1] [14]It was now about noon of the day before Passover. And Pilate said to the Jews, "Here is your king!"

[15]"Away with him," they yelled. "Away with him—crucify him!"

"What? Crucify your king?" Pilate asked.

"We have no king but Caesar," the chief priests shouted back. [16]Then Pilate gave Jesus to them to be crucified.

[17]So they had Him at last, and He was taken out of the city, carrying His cross to the place known as "The Skull," in Hebrew, "Golgotha." [18]There they crucified Him and two others with Him, one on either side with Jesus between them. [19]And Pilate posted a sign above Him reading, "JESUS OF NAZARETH, THE KING OF THE JEWS." [20]The place where Jesus was crucified was near the city; and the signboard was written in Hebrew, Latin and Greek, so that many people read it. [21]Then the chief priests said to Pilate, "Change it from 'The King of the Jews' to '*He said,* I am King of the Jews.'"

[22]Pilate replied, "What I have written, I have written. It stays exactly as it is."

[23,24]When the soldiers had crucified Jesus, they put His garments into four piles, one for each of them. But they said, "Let's not tear up his robe," for it was seamless. "Let's throw dice to see who gets it."

This fulfilled the Scripture that says, "They divided My clothes among them, and cast lots for My robe"[1].

[25]So that is what they did.

Standing near the cross were Jesus' mother, Mary, His aunt, the wife of Cleopas, and Mary Magdalene. [26]When Jesus saw His mother standing beside me, His

198

close friend,ᵏ He said to her, "He is your son." ²⁷And to meˡ He said, "She is your mother!" And from then on Iᵐ took her into my home.

²⁸Jesus knew that everything was now finished, and to fulfill the Scriptures said, "I'm thirsty."

²⁹A jar of sour wine was sitting there, so a sponge was soaked in it and put on a hyssop branch and held up to His lips. ³⁰When Jesus had tasted it, He said, "It is finished," and bowed His head and dismissed His spirit.

³¹The Jewish leaders didn't want the victims hanging there the next day, which was the Sabbath (and a very special Sabbath at that, for it was the Passover), so they asked Pilate to order the legs of the men broken to hasten death; then their bodies could be taken down. ³²So the soldiers came and broke the legs of the two men crucified with Jesus; ³³But when they came to Him; they saw that He was dead already, and they didn't break His legs. ³⁴However, one of the soldiers pierced His side with a spear, and blood and water flowed out. ³⁵I saw this all myself and have given an accurate report so that you also can believe.ⁿ

³⁶,³⁷The soldiers did this in fulfillment of the Scripture that says, "Not one of His bones shall be broken," and, "They shall look on Him whom they pierced."

³⁸Afterwards Joseph of Arimathea, who had been a secret disciple of Jesus for fear of the Jewish leaders, boldly asked Pilate for permission to take Jesus' body down; and Pilate told him to go ahead. So he came and took it away. ³⁹Nicodemus, the man who had come to Jesus at night,° came too, bringing a hundred pounds of embalming ointment made from myrrh and aloes. ⁴⁰Together they wrapped Jesus' body in a long linen cloth saturated with the spices, as is the Jewish custom of burial. ⁴¹The place of crucifixion was near a grove of trees,ᵖ where there was a new tomb, never used before. ⁴²And so, because of the need for haste before the Sabbath, and because the tomb was close at hand, they laid Him there.

Could Jesus have saved Himself?

Much has been written about the crucifixion of Jesus Christ. Some people see it as an unfortunate and unfair crime against an innocent man who was "too good a teacher" for His own good. Others see it as much more than that. Indeed, if it is to be one part of the world's most important event, it would have to be more than the death of a man.

Here are two points of view on the crucifixion: one comes from the eloquent pen of Peter Marshall, one of the most outstanding preachers of all time who served as chaplain to the United States Senate until his death in 1949. In his book, *Mr. Jones, Meet the Master,* Peter Marshall included a sermon, "The Paradox of Salvation":

Peter Marshall's picture of the crucifixion:

Aye, they could admit it now. They could grant him triumphs of yesterday, for now, today, the triumph was theirs!

It was strangely dark. A thunderstorm was blowing up from the mountains and the clouds hid the sun. Women took children by the hand and hurried back to the city. People looked up at the sky and became frightened. It was an uncanny darkness.

They stood blinking at flashes of lightning like daggers of fire.

There were eyes watching this man on the cross ... shifting doubting eyes, eyes through which hell itself was looking, eyes with gloating in them, other eyes that looked and never saw.

Lips were moving ... fierce, fastened lips drawn in thin lines of cruelty ... open lips that vomited blasphemy like craters of hate.

Faces were looking up at him ... white faces, mad faces, twisted and distorted laughing faces ... convulsed faces ... faces jeering and roaring round the foot of the cross.

There was weeping, too, the crying of women and the unashamed sobbing of men.

The wounded flower of Magdala was consoled by that lovely one who once held him in her arms, while the beloved John stood beside them.

Simon of Cyrene from time to time wiped away his tears with the back of his hand. Peter stood on the fringe of the crowd, blinded by hot tears that filled his eyes, while his very heart broke.

They hurled his own words back at him, but they were barbs, dipped in venom and shot from snarling lips, like poisoned arrows.

"He saved others, himself he cannot save. Yes, he healed the cripples. Yes, he gave sight to the blind. He made withered arms whole again. He even brought back the dead, but he cannot save himself."

They shouted until they were hoarse. The noise was so great that only a few of them standing near the cross heard what he said when his lips moved in prayer:

"Father, forgive them, for they know not what they do."

The sun rose higher and higher. Time oozed out like the blood that dripped from the cross ... Jesus opened his eyes and saw his mother standing there, and John beside her.

He called out the name of John, who came closer, and Jesus said: "You will take care of her, John?" ... and John, choked with tears, put his arm around the shoulders of Mary.

Jesus said to his mother: "He will be your son." His lips were parched and he spoke with difficulty. He moved his head uneasily against the hard wood of the cross, as a sick man moves his head on a hot pillow.

The women beneath the cross stood praying for Jesus and for the thieves. The centurion was silent, although every now and then he would look up at Jesus with a strange look on his face. The soldiers were silent too. The gambling was done. They had won ... and lost.*

Here is another account of the crucifixion—not as eloquent as Peter Marshall's. It was written by a "child of the inner-city"; uneducated, no theological expert, possessor of grammar that would leave the

*From *Mr. Jones, Meet the Master*, Peter Marshall, Fleming H. Revell, Inc.

average English teacher in a trauma. But this "tough kid from the city streets" has a refreshing way of telling the story. He tells it "like it is," as far as he is concerned, and perhaps, as we see the crucifixion through his eyes, we might get a clearer glimpse of how it actually was. . .

Bad Friday

The wheels took Jesus up to the governor who had a funny name. It was Pilate. He didn't know nothin' about Jesus, so he took him into his big office and talked with him and asked him lots of questions. Pretty soon he comes out to the people and says, "Jesus is OK. They ain't nothin' wrong with him." The wheels don't like that, so they gets everybody to yell, "Kill him, kill him, he is causin' lots of trouble around here, and everywhere."

This guy Pilate don't want no part of this and he's thinkin' of a way to get out of it. So he says, "This man comes from another place. I'll send him over to Herod." But Jesus didn't give Herod no answers to his questions, and this made Herod mad and he says, "OK, you asked for it." He had a big purple robe put on Jesus and pokes fun at Jesus. But Herod ain't takin' the rap for this one either and sends him back to Pilate. Pilate's wife had a dream about Jesus and she tells Pilate, "You better let him go. He ain't done nothin' so bad that you have to kill him." Pilate wanted to let him go too so he told the people, "We checked Jesus out and he's OK. There's nothin' wrong with him." But the people wanted blood and they start yellin', "If you let him go you'll be in trouble with big daddy in Rome and we'll get you kicked out." Well, this makes Pilate scared so he tried to find another way out. He figures that he's got them trapped with this one. He tells them about a real big crook by name of Barabbas and says, "I'll let one go—Barabbas or Jesus—who will it be?" They all start yellin', "Barabbas." Pilate never thought that they would yell that, and this bugs him plenty. He tries once more to get out of it and says, "What shall I do with Jesus?" The crowd yells back, "Kill him." But Pilate still wants nothin' to do with the whole thing and tells one of his flunkies to bring some water to wash his hands, to show everybody he's washin' his hands of the whole thing. But like all the other politicians he wants to please everybody and he sends some of the army guys to take Jesus away to get killed. They wanted to have some fun with Jesus first, so they put a crown on his head, only it was made of thorns, and then they spit on him and beat on him and did all kinds of nasty things to him. Then the time came and they made him carry the heavy cross that they was gonna kill him on. They was two crooks gettin' killed that day too.

Everybody followed just like it was a big fireman's carnival or somethin' like that. Jesus had taken such a beatin' that he passed out, and the army guys grabbed one of the crowd to carry the cross and that was the only good thing they did all day long. When they got to the top of the hill they stripped Jesus and the two crooks and put them on the crosses and pounded nails in their hands. Then they put up the crosses and waited for them to die. The army guys sold chances on his clothes.

Pretty soon Jesus says, "Don't be too hard on them, Father, they been led on by the crowd. They don't know what the score is."

Then they put up a sign. It says "King of the Jews."

About that time one of the crooks was hurtin' real bad and he started swearin' and makin' fun of Jesus. The other crook he don't want no part of that and tells the first crook to shut up, "The guy in the middle ain't done nothin' like we have. We got what's comin' to us, but he's OK." Then he turns to Jesus and says, "Don't forget me and put in a good word for me later." Jesus tells him, "Don't worry about it—you're already with me."

The real sad part of this whole horrible mess was that his mother had to watch what was goin' on. But even then he didn't forget his mother and he tells John to take care of her.

By this time it's gettin' real dark and it lasted about three hours. Then when everything was quiet Jesus lets out a real hollow and says, "That's it, it's all over," and he died. One of the army guys standin' near the grave says, 'You know what I think? He *was* God's son, that's what.' "*

*From God Is for Real, Man, Carl F. Burke, chaplain of Erie County Jail, Buffalo, New York. Copyright 1966, Association Press, p. 98.

For one more thought on the crucifixion, return for a moment to Peter Marshall's sermon on "The Paradox of Salvation." The crowd had sneered and shouted at Jesus saying that "He saved others, Himself He cannot save!" Was the crowd right? Peter Marshall puts it this way:

". . . they were wrong, as well as right. Could he not have saved himself?

"He might have compromised with the priests—made a bargain with Caiaphas, talked things over with Pilate. He might have made his kingdom political instead of spiritual.

"He might have chosen the expedient rather than the right. As he himself reminded Peter, he might have called upon twelve legions of angels to rescue him and to show his great power.

"He might have withstood the plottings and devices of wicked men. Yes, he might have saved himself. He had the power; but then he would never have been our Savior! For no man can save himself who saves another.

"Such is the paradox of salvation!

"The acorn cannot save itself, if it is to bud a tree. The soldier cannot save himself, if he is to save his country. Nor can the Shepherd save himself, if he would save his sheep.

HE MIGHT HAVE SAVED HIMSELF, BUT THEN HE NEVER WOULD HAVE BEEN OUR SAVIOUR

"Christ is the Good Shepherd, and hence, when he would consummate the great salvation, there was no other way to save us than to lay down his life for our salvation.

"For to love is never to think of one's self, but to give one's self for the one loved.

"And he loved us and gave himself for us." *

And so Jesus died, and that was the end of that. Or so most people thought. . .

John 20:1-31

[1]Early Sunday[q] morning, while it was still dark, Mary Magdalene came to the tomb and found that the stone was rolled aside from the entrance. [2]She ran and found Simon Peter and me[r] and said, "They have taken the Lord's body out of the tomb, and I don't know where they have put Him!"

[3,4]We[s] ran to the tomb to see; I[t] outran Peter and got there first, [5]and stooped and looked in and saw the linen cloth lying there, but I didn't go in. [6]Then Simon Peter arrived and went on inside. He also noticed the cloth lying there, [7]while the swath that had covered Jesus' head was rolled up in a bundle and was lying at the side. [8]Then I[u] went in, too, and saw, and believed [that He had risen]—[9]For until then we hadn't realized that the Scriptures said He would come to life again! [10]We[v] went on home,

[11]And by that time Mary had returned to the tomb[w] and was standing outside crying. And as she wept, she stooped and looked in [12]And saw two white-robed angels sitting at the head and foot of the place where the body of Jesus had been lying.

[13]"Why are you crying?" the angels asked her.

"Because they have taken away my Lord," she replied, "and I don't know where they have put Him."

[14]She glanced over her shoulder and saw someone standing behind her. It was Jesus, but she didn't recognize Him!

*From *Mr. Jones, Meet the Master*, Peter Marshall, Fleming H. Revell, Inc.

[15]"Why are you crying?" He asked her. "Whom are you looking for?"

(She thought He was the gardener.) "Sir," she said, "if you have taken Him away, tell me where you have put Him, and I will go and get Him."

[16]"Mary!" Jesus said. She turned toward Him.

"Master!" she exclaimed.

[17]"Don't touch Me," He cautioned, "for I haven't yet ascended to the Father. But go find My brothers and tell them that I ascend to My Father and your Father, My God and your God."

[18]Mary Magdalene found the disciples and told them, "I have seen the Lord!" Then she gave them His message.

[19]That evening the disciples were meeting behind locked doors, in fear of the Jewish leaders, when suddenly Jesus was standing there among them! After greeting them, [20]He showed them His hands and side. And how wonderful was their joy as they saw their Lord!

[21]He spoke to them again and said, "As the Father has sent Me, even so I am sending you."

[22]Then He breathed on them, and told them, "Receive the Holy Spirit! [23]If you forgive anyone's sins, they are forgiven. If you refuse to forgive them, they are unforgiven."

[24]One of the disciples, Thomas "The Twin," was not there at the time with the others. [25]When they kept telling him, "We have seen the Lord," he replied, "I won't believe it unless I see the nail wounds in His hands—and put my fingers into them—and place my hand into His side."

[26]Eight days later the disciples were together again, and this time Thomas was with them. The doors were locked; but suddenly, as before, Jesus was standing among them and greeting them.

[27]Then He said to Thomas, "Put your finger into My hands. Put your hand into My side. Don't be faithless any longer. Believe!"

Theories that try to "explain" the resurrection

Some people have not wanted to believe the Biblical account of the resurrection, so they offer various theories to explain the empty tomb. One of these is the fraud theory, which claims someone stole the body of Jesus to make it appear that He rose from the dead.

The answer to the fraud theory lies in the fact that Pilate posted Roman guards at the tomb. We read in Matthew 28 that the Jewish leaders bribed these guards to say someone stole the body while they slept. If the guards were asleep, how could they be sure of what happened? An even stronger argument against the fraud theory is the martyrdom suffered by the disciples for their faith in Christ. People do not die for the sake of a fraud.

Another false explanation of the empty tomb is the swoon theory, which claims Jesus never really died. He supposedly lost consciousness on the cross and was put in the tomb. Later He "came to" and escaped.

Answers to the swoon theory are many. The Gospel accounts report terrible wounds suffered by Jesus (John 19:30-37). A spear was thrust into his side by a Roman soldier. Also, there is this question: how could a man with nail wounds in his hands and feet and a spear wound in his side move a heavy stone and walk away?

Another false explanation of the empty tomb is the ghost theory, which maintains the disciples imagined they saw Jesus in some kind of vision. This theory holds that the disciples wanted Jesus to be alive so much that they produced a subjective image of Him in their mind's eye.

Answers to this theory include: The disciples were not the "vision-seeing type" and they were certainly not in the "vision-seeing mood" following the resurrection. They did not expect the resurrection; they scattered in haste and unbelief and hid away in fear of the authorities. Furthermore, when Jesus appeared to the 11 in the upper room (Luke 24:36-43) He ate with them and invited them to touch Him to find out that He had flesh and bones.

Unbelieving people may argue their pet theories on the resurrection, but the plain statement of facts in the Bible still remains. No one has disproven the Biblical account. The only explanation for the empty tomb is the resurrection of the body of the Lord Jesus Christ.

207

[28]"My Lord and my God!" Thomas said.

[29]Then Jesus told him, "You believe because you have seen Me. But blessed are those who haven't seen Me and believe anyway."

[30,31]Jesus' disciples saw Him do many other miracles besides the ones told about in this book, but these are recorded so that you will believe that He is the Messiah, the Son of God, and that believing in Him you will have Life.

How to start a new religion

Two French gentlemen were talking—Monsieur Lepeaux and the statesman-bishop Talleyrand, who became a leader of the French revolution. Lepeaux was quite disappointed at his failure to gain followers for his new religion, which he regarded as an improvement on Christianity. He explained that despite all efforts by himself and his supporters, his propaganda gained no converts. He finally asked Talleyrand what he should do.

Talleyrand replied that it was indeed difficult to found a new religion, more difficult indeed than

ANYONE CAN START A NEW RELIGION IF...

could be imagined, so difficult that he hardly knew what to advise.

"Still," said Talleyrand after a moment's reflection, "There is one plan that you might at least try. I should recommend you to be crucified and to rise again on the third day."*

TAKE TIME . . .

The cock crows on schedule. Read John 18:1-27. Why do you think Simon Peter was willing to draw his sword and start slashing away in the garden (v. 10) but then he turned into a cowardly liar in the court outside the high priest's house where Jesus' so-called trial was going on? Did denying Christ make a better man of Peter or a weaker one? Why?

What is truth? Read John 18:28-40. Why does Pilate ask Jesus "What is truth?" What did this tell you about Pilate? What is your own answer to the question "What is truth?"

The real Pontius Pilate stands up. Read John 19:1-16. This is an interesting study in the struggle in one man's mind between justice and his concern for his own skin. Pilate knew full well that Jesus was guilty of no crime. But yet he sent Jesus to death on the cross. What made Pilate "sell Jesus out"? What makes a Christian "sell Jesus out" today in some situations?

So they crucified Him . . . Read John 19:17-27. There is a poignant scene in these verses. Jesus makes sure that His mother will be cared for by John, His beloved disciple. Here in the midst of the pain and the horror involved in redeeming all mankind from sin, Jesus takes time to take care of a tender detail. What does this tell you about Jesus' humanity? What does this tell you about God's love for mankind and His involvement with man? Does this scene seem to make God far away or rather close? Why?

It is finished. Read John 19:28-42. Nicodemus was in the crowd watching Jesus die, and Nicodemus came forward later to help claim His body. What do you think Nicodemus

*Account of Talleyrand's meeting with Lepeaux adapted from a report in *Studies on the Resurrection of Christ* by Charles H. Robinson, which was reprinted in *Decision*, March 1964.

must have thought when Jesus uttered the final words, "It is finished"?

I have seen the Lord! Read John 20:1-18. Note v. 8—John saw that Jesus' body was gone and believed that He had risen. What else do you think John believed? That is, what did Jesus' resurrection confirm for John? What does it confirm for every Christian?

My Lord and my God! Read John 20:19-31. Because he expressed doubt when his fellow disciples told him of Christ's resurrection, Thomas gained a label of derision that has come down with him to this day—the "doubting Thomas." But aren't all of us a little bit like Thomas (or perhaps a great deal like Thomas)? Thomas doubted, true, but he also was quick to confess Jesus as Lord and God when he did see the evidence. Have we done the same? Think this last question over in the light of John 20:31.

TAKE INVENTORY . . .

Ask yourself the question, "What is the truth?" What is your answer? Think carefully about this; don't rattle off some good "spiritual" answer. With all of the knowledge available today . . . with all of the philosophies being practiced . . . with all of the "self-discovery" religions and ideologies being tried the question "What is truth?" is no light matter. Does truth center for you in a set of doctrines or Biblical precepts, or does it center in a person, Jesus Christ?

Do you believe the resurrection really happened? That is, that Jesus actually did "rise from the dead," that His body came back to life and that He conquered the grave? Many people talk about the resurrection, but many of these same people don't really believe it. But if a Christian really doubts there is a resurrection, how can he "tell it like it is" between him and his Lord?

TAKE ACTION . . .

Talk to someone (Christian or non-Christian, or possibly both) about the crucifixion and the resurrection. See how much they really know about these events and share with them your feelings about "the most important event in history." Do they agree that it is? If you believe that it is, give them your reasons for saying so.

CHAPTER 16

So . . . stay near the door

Chapter 21 of John's Gospel is called an "epilogue," and so it is, because the Gospel story seems to have ended with the 20th chapter. But isn't there some unfinished business between Jesus and His disciples? That unfinished business is taken care of in this account. The disciples go off to fish, they have no luck, and then they meet a "stranger" on the shore. The stranger turns out to be their Lord, Who invites them to breakfast. And then Jesus turns to Peter—Simon the Rock, who had crumbled rather easily in the face of opposition just a few days before. Will Jesus give Peter a tongue lashing? No, but He has something to say to Peter—and something to say to anyone who knows Christ as Saviour and wants to "tell it like it is". . .

211

¹Later Jesus appeared again to the disciples beside the Lake of Galilee. This is how it happened: ²A group of us were there—Simon Peter, Thomas "The Twin," Nathanael from Cana in Galilee, my brother James and Iˣ and two other disciples. ³Simon Peter said, "I'm going fishing."

"We'll come too," we all said. We did, but caught nothing all night. ⁴At dawn we saw a man standing on the beach but couldn't see who he was.

⁵He called, "Any fish, boys?"ʸ

"No," we replied.

⁶Then He said, "Throw out your net on the righthand side of the boat, and you'll get plenty of them!" So we did, and couldn't draw in the net because of the weight of the fish, there were so many!

⁷Then Iˣ said to Peter, "It is the Lord!" At that, Simon Peter put on his tunic (for he was stripped to the waist) and jumped into the water [and swam ashoreᵃ].

⁸The rest of us stayed in the boat and pulled the loaded net to the beach, about 300 feet away. ⁹When we got there, we saw that a fire was kindled and fish were frying over it, and there was bread. ¹⁰"Bring some of the fish you've just caught," Jesus said.

¹¹So Simon Peter went out and dragged the net ashore. By his count there were 153 large fish; and yet the net hadn't torn!

¹²"Now come and have some breakfast!" Jesus said; and none of us dared ask Him if He really was the Lord, for we were quite sure of it.

¹³Then Jesus went around serving us the bread and fish. ¹⁴This was the third time Jesus had appeared to us since His return from the dead.

¹⁵After breakfast Jesus said to Simon Peter, "Simon, son of John, do you love Me more than these others?"ᵇ

"Yes," Peter replied, "You know I am Your friend."

"Then feed My lambs," Jesus told him.

[16]Jesus repeated the question: "Simon, son of John, do you *really* love Me?"

"Yes, Lord," Peter said, "You know I am Your friend."

"Then take care of My sheep," Jesus said.

[17]Once more He asked him, "Simon, son of John, are you even My friend?"

Peter was grieved at the way Jesus asked the question this third time. "Lord, You know my heart;[c] You know I am," he said.

Jesus said, "Then feed My little sheep.

[18]"When you were young, you were able to do as you liked and go wherever you wanted to; but when you are old, you will stretch out your hands and others will direct you and take you where you don't want to go."

[19]Jesus said this to let him know what kind of death he would die to glorify God. Then Jesus told him, "Follow Me."

[20]Peter turned around and saw the disciple Jesus loved following, the one who had leaned around at supper that time to ask Jesus, "Master, which of us will betray You?" [21]Peter asked Jesus, "What about him, Lord? What sort of death will he die?"[d]

[22]Jesus replied, "If I want him to live[e] until I return, what is that to you? *You* follow Me."

[23]So the rumor spread among the brotherhood that that disciple wouldn't die! But that isn't what Jesus said at all! He only said, "If I want him to live until I come, what is that to you?"

[24]*I am that disciple!* I saw these events and have recorded them here. And we all know that my account of these things is accurate. [25]And I suppose that if all the other events in Jesus' life were written, the whole world could hardly contain the books!

Do you love Him more than "these"?

There is an interesting thing about Scripture: God usually says a thing only once, and that should be enough for anyone. But here in John 21, He says the same thing three times. It would seem that we should pay especially close attention.

Put yourself in Peter's place at this early morning breakfast on the Sea of Galilee. It must have been a lovely time with a new day just dawning, the sun beginning to peep through, and the Lord Himself there to break bread with His disciples. But Peter probably wasn't enjoying it too much. There was a gap between him and his Lord now. He had failed Jesus; he had denied Him three times just as Jesus said he would. There was a great wound in their relationship and it had to be healed. And so, the Lord applied three dressings to that wound.

Three times He asked Peter if Peter really loved Him, was really His friend. Three times, Peter assured Him that this was so and three times Jesus said, "Then feed My sheep."

It is as if Jesus is telling Peter: "You denied Me once, Peter, but there are better days ahead as long as you face them with one goal in mind: To feed My sheep, to share Me with others, to communicate the Gospel wherever you go."

And what about Christians today? The Lord asks the same question: "Do you love Me more than these?" "These" might mean anything. it might mean the Christian's family, the Christian's talents, his job, his possessions. But unless you love Christ more than "any of these" you will not possess the power to "feed His sheep."

Dr. Samuel Shoemaker, called by *Newsweek* magazine one of America's ten most outstanding preachers, devoted his life to "feeding Christ's sheep." Besides pastoring parishes in New York and Pittsburgh, he was a spiritual pioneer who formed the seed ground of Alcoholics Anonymous. He also was instrumental in the founding of such organizations as the Fellowship of Christian Athletes, Young Life, and *Faith at Work* magazine. From 1945 until his death in 1963, Dr. Shoemaker carried on a weekly broadcast, "Your Life Today" over station WJZ of New York City. A prolific writer, he authored 26 books, many pamphlets, and many articles.

For those who have been stirred by reading the Gospel of John and the many accounts of personal experiences with Christ . . . for those who feel committed to communicating Christ—to "telling it like it is" . . . for those who know they love Christ and who want to feed His sheep, here is what Dr. Shoemaker called "An Apologia for My Life." In these inspired lines of free-flowing verse is a matchless creed for any Christian witness who sees a needy world that wants to hear someone "tell it like it is."

So I Stay Near the Door

I stay near the door.
I neither go too far in, nor stay too far out,
The door is the most important door in the world—
It is the door through which men walk when they
    find God.
There's no use my going way inside, and staying there,
When so many are still outside and they, as much as I,
Crave to know where the door is.
And all that so many ever find
Is only the wall where a door ought to be.
They creep along the wall like blind men,

With outstretched, groping hands,
Feeling for a door, knowing there must be a door,
Yet they never find it...
So I stay near the door.

The most tremendous thing in the world
Is for men to find that door—the door to God.
The most important thing any man can do
Is to take hold of one of those blind, groping hands,
And put it on the latch—the latch that only clicks
And opens to the man's own touch.
Men die outside that door, as starving beggars die
On cold nights in cruel cities in the dead of winter—
Die for want of what is within their grasp.
They live, on the other side of it—live because they
    have found it.
Nothing else matters compared to helping them find it,
And open it, and walk in, and find Him...
So I stay near the door.

Go in, great saints, go all the way in—
Go way down into the cavernous cellars,
And way up into the spacious attics—
It is a vast, roomy house, this house where God is.
Go into the deepest of hidden casements,
Of withdrawal, of silence, of sainthood.
Some must inhabit those inner rooms,
And know the depths and heights of God,
And call outside to the rest of us how wonderful it is.
Sometimes I take a deeper look in,
Sometimes venture in a little farther;
But my place seems closer to the opening...
So I stay near the door.

There is another reason why I stay there.
Some people get part way in and become afraid
Lest God and the zeal of His house devour them;
For God is so very great, and asks all of us.
And these people feel a cosmic claustrophobia,

And want to get out. "Let me out!" they cry.
And the people way inside only terrify them more.
Somebody must be by the door to tell them that they
    are spoiled
For the old life, they have seen too much:
Once taste God, and nothing but God will do anymore.
Somebody must be watching for the frightened
Who seek to sneak out just where they came in,
To tell them how much better it is inside.
The people too far in do not see how near these are
To leaving—preoccupied with the wonder of it all.
Somebody must watch for those who have entered the
    door,
But would like to run away. So for them, too
I stay near the door.

I admire the people who go way in.
But I wish they would not forget how it was
Before they got in. Then they would be able to help
The people who have not yet even found the door,
Or the people who want to run away again from God.
You can go in too deeply, and stay in too long,
And forget the people outside the door.
As for me, I shall take my old accustomed place,
Near enough to God to hear Him, and know He is
    there,
But not so far from men as not to hear them,
And remember they are there, too.
Where? Outside the door—
Thousands of them, millions of them.
But—more important for me—
One of them, two of them, ten of them,
Whose hands I am intended to put on the latch.
So I shall stay by the door and wait
For those who seek it.
"I had rather be a door-keeper. . ."*
So I stay near the door.

*From *Extraordinary Living for Ordinary Men,* Samuel Shoemaker,
Zondervan Publishing House, 1965, p. 158.

How to Witness

By Paul E. Little. Copyright 1966,
Inter-Varsity Press. Used by permission.

What do we mean by "witnessing"? Spouting a lot ot
Bible verses to a non-Christian? Not quite. "Witnessing"
involves all that we are and therefore do; it goes far beyond
what we say at certain inspired moments. So the question
is not *will* we witness (speak), but *how* will we witness?
When we're trusting Jesus Christ as Lord as well as
Savior, He enables us to live and speak as faithful witnesses.

From our Lord's interview with the Samaritan woman at
a well near Sychar, for instance, we may discover some
practical, basic principles to follow as we try to represent
Him in a realistic, natural way.

Contact others socially

*When the Lord knew that the Pharisees had heard about
the greater crowds coming to Him than to John to be
baptized and to become His disciples—(though Jesus
Himself didn't baptize them, but His disciples did)—He
left Judea and returned to the province of Galilee. He had
to go through Samaria on the way, and around noon as He
approached the village of Sychar, He came to Jacob's Well,
located on the parcel of ground Jacob gave to his son
Joseph. Jesus was tired from the long walk in the hot sun
and sat wearily beside the well. Soon a Samaritan woman
came to draw water . . .* (John 4:1-7, Living New Testament.)

The first principle is obvious: we must have social
contact with non-Christians. Yet it is being ignored in many
Christian circles. This simple fact explains a lot of the
apparent powerlessness of the Gospel in today's world.
Both in our Christian groups (churches and otherwise) and
as individuals, we often see no one come to Jesus Christ
because no non-Christians are listening to our message.
The Holy Spirit can't save saints or seats. If we don't know
any non-Christians, how can we introduce them to the
Savior?

When our Lord called Simon and Andrew, He said, "Follow me and I will make you become fishers of men" (Mark 1:17). Among other things He was teaching that to catch fish one must go where fish are. A simple Simon with his line in a barrel is a pathetic figure. Yet some of us seem to be just that in evangelism. We hold evangelistic meetings with few or no non-Christians present! The fish avoid our barrel in droves. We must go where they are if we are to gain any significant audience for the Gospel.

Much of our difficulty stems from falsely equating separation and isolation. A medical analogy may help us. When the Department of Health fears an epidemic of scarlet fever, it tries to isolate the germ-carriers. If everyone who has the disease is quarantined the disease won't spread. Similarly, a sure preventive against the spread of the Gospel is to isolate its carriers (Christians) from everyone else. The enemy of mankind attempts to do just that by persuading us to clan together and avoid all unnecessary contact with non-Christians, lest we contaminate ourselves. By his devilish logic he has convinced many Christians. Some have informed me with evident pride that no non-Christian has ever been inside their home. Feeling very spiritual, they have boasted that they have no non-Christian friends. And then they wonder why they've never had the joy of introducing someone to the Savior!

Let's repeat this *first principle for witnessing—be in contact with non-Christians.* We should each ask ourselves, "For whom am I praying by name every day, asking God the Holy Spirit to open his eyes, enlighten him, and bend his will until he receives Jesus Christ as Lord and Savior? Is there any one person with whom I am seeking opportunities to show the love of Christ? Am I willing to take the further initiative to communicate the Gospel to him as the Spirit gives opportunity?" If we discover an absence of vital contact with non-Christians, we may simply ask God to show us one person whom He wants us to befriend, pray for, love, and eventually bring to the Savior, and He will show us that one. "Lift up your eyes and see ..." He says (John 4:35).

Establish a common interest

Then we can apply the second principle: establish a common interest as a bridge for communication. Let's look back at the passage:

219

*Soon a Samaritan woman came to draw water, and Jesus
asked her for a drink. He was alone at the time as His
disciples had gone into the village to buy some food* (John
4:7,8, Living New Testament).

We Christians tend to pooh-pooh anything that calls for
much preliminary preparation. We like to skip the "non-es-
sentials" and get right to the point. Preludes are a waste of
time, or so we think. If I'd been our Lord, I'd probably
have blurted out immediatly, "Lady, do you know who I
am?" Our Lord didn't approach her that way. In this
incident He began by referring to something in which she
was obviously interested. (She'd come to draw water.)
Gradually He directed the conversation away from this
known interest to a spiritual reality which she knew
nothing about. Most people resent being trapped in a
one-way conversation by someone who moves in and
expounds his theme without even bothering to find out if
the listener is interested. We resent it, too. It makes us
start wondering if the speaker cares about us at all or if he
just wants to hear his favorite little speech again.

I wish I'd learned this lesson about communicating with
people sooner. About once every six months the pressure to
witness used to reach explosive heights inside me. Not
knowing any better, I would suddenly lunge at someone
and spout all my verses with a sort of glazed stare in my
eye. I honestly didn't expect any response. As soon as my
victim indicated lack of interest, I'd begin to edge away
from him with a sigh of relief and the consoling thought,
"All that will live godly in Christ Jesus shall suffer
persecution" (II Timothy 3:12). Duty done, I'd draw back
into my martyr's shell for another six months' hibernation,
until the internal pressure again became intolerable and
drove me out. It really shocked me when I finally realized
that I, not the cross, was offending people. My inept,
unwittingly rude, even stupid approach to them was re-
sponsible for their rejection of me and the Gospel message.

As instruments in God's hands, we must work positively
and patiently to establish mutual interests with others,
beginning first where their interests lie. Later on we can
profitably discuss spiritual matters together. Dale Carne-
gie's popular book, *How to Win Friends and Influence
People*, offers many apt illustrations of human personality
in action and reaction, along with some sane, common-
sense suggestions for improving our relationships with

people.* For instance, he reminds us that the voice any person likes to hear best is his own. Everyone likes to talk, but some do more than others. Many people would give anything to find someone who would just listen to them. When we listen long enough, we not only begin to know and understand an individual; we also gain his gratitude and his willingness to listen to us, enabling us later to speak relevantly to him. In this way the Holy Spirit often draws men to us and then through us tells them about Jesus Christ so that they themselves may come to Him.

Arouse curiosity

As we read on in John 4 we can see our Lord arousing the woman's interest and curiosity in His message through two means:

The woman was surprised that a Jew would ask a "despised Samaritan" for anything—usually they wouldn't even speak to them!—and she remarked about this to Jesus. He replied, "If you only knew what a wonderful gift God has for you, and who I am, you would ask Me for some living water!"

"But you don't have a rope or a bucket," she said, "and this is a very deep well! From where would you get this living water? And besides, are you greater than our ancestor Jacob? How can you offer better water than this which he and his sons and cattle enjoyed?"

Jesus replied that people soon became thirsty again after drinking this water. "But the water I give them," He said, "becomes a perpetual spring within them, watering them forever with eternal life."

"Please, sir," the woman said, "give me some of that water! Then I'll never be thirsty again and won't have to make this long trip out here every day." (John 4:9-15, Living New Testament)

It is fascinating to see this woman's curiosity kindled and beginning to burn as our Lord draws her along. First, He came to her where she was. Second, He showed an interest in her concerns. Now, He is using his actions and His words to arouse a positive response to Himself and His message of truth.

*Because this book is based on a selfish motivation (which characterizes much of our society today), i.e., how to get your hand into another man's pocket, I cannot recommend it on ethical grounds. But despite its ethics, it can help us understand people better.

221

At this point, the impact of His action lies merely in His speaking at all. By this simple act of talking with the woman, He demolishes social, religious, and racial-political barriers. As a man He speaks to her, a woman. As a Rabbi He speaks to her, an immoral woman. As a Jew He speaks to her, a Samaritan. Thus He startles her. While she can't quite grasp His significance, she can sense the deeper dimension in His life by His refusal to discriminate against her. He is accepting her.

In following our Lord's example, how should we try to gain people's attention and interest so that God may, through us, bring them to conviction and decision? I personally believe that parading along the sidewalk in a sandwich board which reads in large, scrawly letters, "I'm a Christian. Ask me" is not the Lord's method. He did not call us to become oddballs. As we represent Christ some people *will* think we are fools, and they will tell us so, but their opinion does not give us license to indulge in bizarre behavior. Oddballism may momentarily arouse curiosity about us, but it tends to discourage true interest in the Gospel.

That deeper, other dimension of life—which non-Christians lack but can usually recognize—should characterize us as Christians. As we spend time with a non-Christian, our sense of real purpose in life, the values we hold, those things that really consume us and our energies will reveal themselves naturally in our everyday activities. Attitudes toward people, reactions to circumstances, that quiet peace and contentment which upholds us in the midst of all life's pressures and crises will suggest the quality of our lives. If we are no different than the people around us in these areas, we need, in the Lord's presence, to determine what is missing and then ask Him to meet our need.

If our lives are full of inconsistencies, we'd better keep our mouths shut. However, I'm not suggesting that we wait for perfection before we speak to anyone. Satan wants to keep us quiet. One of his deceitful methods is the attempt to convince us that we mustn't witness to anyone about Jesus Christ until we're good enough to pass for Gabriel's twin. After all, we mustn't be hypocrites. This lie that we need perfection before speaking has silenced many Christians. Actually, the personal weaknesses and failings we feel most keenly are seldom noticed by the person who doesn't know Jesus Christ. For as we go along in genuine daily fellowship with Jesus Christ, the Holy Spirit both convicts us of sin and adds that other dimension to our lives—even though we may not feel it there. Like Moses whose face shone so brightly, others will see this quality in our lives far more readily than we ourselves can. And their curiosity may lead them beyond what we are to inquire about the source of our life in Christ.

Sometimes the question is asked, "Which is more important in witnessing, the life I live or the words I say?" This question throws the consistency of our lives and our verbal witness into a false antithesis. It's like asking which wing of an airplane is more important, the right or the left! Obviously both are essential and you don't have anything without both. Life and lip are inseparable in an effective witness to Christ.

Since, in reacting against high-pressure evangelism, many of us tend toward a passive silence, we need to learn how to be aggressive spokesmen for the Lord without being obnoxious. Our Lord teased the Samaritan woman into asking a question by what He said. This is a principle we may follow also. Once the non-Christian takes the first step in initiative, all pressure goes out of any conversation about Jesus Christ. It can be picked up at the point where it is left without embarrassment. On the other hand, so long as we are forcing our way against increasing resistance we tend to do far more harm than good. How can we get a non-Christian to ask a question? The answer is by throwing out bait as fishers of men and speaking to those who respond.

We cannot create spiritual interest in the life of anyone, even though we might like to. Only the Holy Spirit can do this. However, we can be instruments in His hand to uncover the interest that He has put there. We will discover so many people who are interested in spiritual reality that we won't have to force ourselves on people who are not interested. It is an enormous relief when we discover that we can legitimately drop the subject if, after throwing out the bait, we do not discover a response prompted by the Holy Spirit.

Every person I have known who has been used of God in personal evangelism has had an attitude of expectancy to discover interested people. In any group of people or in conversation with any particular individual he asks himself the question, "Lord, is this one in whom you are working?"

and then, as the Spirit gives opportunity, he proceeds to see what the response is.

Relieved of the tension of forced conversation with an unwilling listener, we can talk then and later about Jesus Christ. Confident of the Lord's guidance and freed from the sense of pressure or embarrassment, we will be natural as we introduce spiritual things.

But how do we throw out bait? Our Lord did it by making a cryptic statement precipitating a question from the Samaritan woman. His statement related to her primary needs and at the same time suggested His ability and willingness to meet those needs.

"If you only knew what a wonderful gift God has for you, and who I am, you would ask Me for some living water!"

"But you don't have a rope or a bucket," she said, "and this is a very deep well! From where would you get this living water? And besides are you greater than our ancestor Jacob?" (John 4:10-12, Living New Testament)

We might make a statement or first ask a leading question ourselves. Jesus also anticipated the woman's reactions. Her questions did not catch Him off guard even once. To take full advantage of each opportunity, we also need to consider the likely responses. As we think about possible situations, let's think through how to throw out the bait and how to handle the likely response.

After even a vague reference to "religion" in a conversation, many Christians have used this practical series of questions to draw out latent spiritual interest: First, "By the way, are you interested in spiritual things?" Many will say, "Yes." But even if the person says, "No," we can ask a second question, "What do you think a real Christian is?" Wanting to hear *his* opinion invariably pleases a person. From his response we'll also gain a more accurate, first-hand—if perhaps shocking—understanding of his thinking as a non-Christian; and because we have listened to him, he'll be much more ready to listen to us. Answers to this question usually revolve around some external action—going to church, reading the Bible, praying, tithing, being baptized. After such an answer we can agree that a real Christian usually *does* these things, but then point out that that's not what a real Christian *is*. A real Christian is one who is personally related to Jesus Christ as a living Person. If the non-Christian continues to indicate interest as we explain this, we can go on to the third question, "Would you like to become a real Christian now?" An amazing number of people today are drifting in a spiritual fog, yearning for someone to lead them into spiritual certainty.

If we are talking to a friend of Roman Catholic background, we might remark, "You know, I have a lot more in common with you than I do with my liberal Protestant friends." He may be surprised by this comment but it will gratify him. We can then explain, "You believe in the Bible as the Word of God, in the deity of Christ, in the necessity of His death as an atonement for our sins, and in His resurrection from the dead; but many liberal Protestants deny these basic facts of New Testament Christianity." We can then go on to say, "I suppose that in the Catholic Church you've discovered the same thing that I see in the Protestant Church: Some Methodists, Baptists, Presbyterians, Episcopalians, etc. really know Jesus Christ personally, and some don't." Invariably he will agree and thus recognize a major fact, namely that church membership in any church does not, in itself, guarantee a personal relationship with Jesus Christ. We can then discuss with him what it means to be personally related to the Lord.

In these and similar situations, knowing what we are going to say beforehand will help overcome nervousness and put us at ease. If we clutch, the other person clutches; but if we relax, he relaxes. As we gain in quiet confidence that the Holy Spirit will lead us to interested people, we can overcome any tendency to be apologetic about our faith. When we assume lack of interest by someone we tend to defeat ourselves before we start. On the other hand, if we assume interest we will usually get an interested response. Each successful encounter with a non-Christian will lead us to greater faith and confidence for the next one.

Don't go too far

The next part of our Lord's conversation reveals principles four and five: give a person only as much of the message as he is ready for, and don't condemn him.

Jesus replied that people soon became thirsty again after drinking this water. "But the water I give them," He said, "becomes a perpetual spring within them, watering them forever with eternal life."

"Please, sir," the woman said, "give me some of that

*water! Then I'll never be thirsty again and won't have to
make this long trip out here every day."*

"Go and get your husband," Jesus told her.

"But I'm not married," the woman replied.

*"All too true!" Jesus said. "For you have had five
husbands, and you aren't even married to the man you're
living with now. [You couldn't have spoken a truer word!]"*

"Sir," the woman said, "You must be a prophet." (John
4:13-19, Living New Testament)

Despite her obvious interest and curiosity, Jesus didn't
give her the whole story at once. Gradually, as she was
ready for more, He revealed more about Himself. Then
when her curiosity had reached fever pitch (v. 26) He
identified Himself as the Christ.

The moment we detect a faint glimmer of interest in a
non-Christian many of us want to rush right in and rattle
off the whole Gospel without coming up for air or waiting to
sense audience response. (After all, we might not get
another chance, we think!) But by relying on the power and
presence of the Holy Spirit, we can gain poise. The
non-Christian needs gentle coaxing when he's just beginning to show his interest: it's usually fragile at first.
Otherwise, like a bird scared from a close-up perch by too
rapid movement toward him, he will withdraw before our
overly eager approach. On the other hand, if we are casual
in our attitude and relaxed in our manner, the inquirer will
tend to press us all the harder to get at the source of our
quiet assurance.

Don't condemn

In the fifth principle we see that our Lord did not
condemn the woman. As she answered Him about her
husband, her sin itself condemned her. In the similar
incident with the woman taken in adultery whom the
self-righteous Pharisees brought to our Lord, Jesus said
"Neither do I condemn you; go, and do not sin again"
(John 8:11). Most of us, on the other hand, are quick to
condemn. Often we have the mistaken idea that if we do
not condemn a certain attitude or deed, we will be condoning it. But this was not our Lord's opinion.

Unwittingly we condemn the non-Christian who offers us
a cigarette, invites us to join him for a drink, or suggests
some other activity that we consider out of bounds. Our

reply may have devastating effects. It is almost reflex action sometimes to say, "No thank you, I don't smoke, drink, etc. I'm a Christian." Mentally we chalk up another point on our testimony scoreboard. What we've actually accomplished is this: we've condemned the person and garbled the Gospel with the false implication that this particular "don't" is an inherent part of Christianity.

How, then, should we answer the non-Christian whose personal customs and convictions differ from ours? The key is to recognize the compliment and generosity implicit in his offer or invitation and to decline on a personal basis so the person doesn't feel condemned or rejected. One way to say "No thanks" on a personal basis is to suggest an alternative activity. When invited to go out for a beer we might answer, "No thanks, but I'll have a coke with you sometime." Or if asked to go somewhere we'd rather not go we could respond, "Thanks, I'm not interested in that, but let me know when you're going to a concert (game, club meeting, etc.) and I'll go with you." By your suggesting an alternative the person realizes you're not rejecting him.

In declining an offer, we don't need to apologize. After all, plenty of non-Christians don't drink, smoke, dance, chew or do certain other things. If a non-Christian isn't interested in playing chess he doesn't blush, hem and haw, and finally mumble apologetically, "No thanks, I don't play chess. I'm a non-Christian." Of course not. He replies breezily, "No thanks, chess leaves me cold. But let me know when you want to play ping pong." As witnesses of Jesus Christ we can and should say "No thanks" in this same easy unembarrassed spirit.

Stick with the main issue

As the interview between our Lord and the Samaritan woman draws to a close, we note two final principles that apply to our witnessing conversations:

"But say, tell me, why is it that you Jews insist that Jerusalem is the only place of worship, while we Samaritans claim it is here [at Mount Gerazim], where our ancestors worshiped?"

Jesus replied, "The time is coming, Ma'am, when we will no longer be concerned about whether to worship the Father here or in Jerusalem. For it's not where we worship that counts, but how we worship—is our worship spiritual

227

and real? Do we have the Holy Spirit's help? For God is Spirit, and we must have His help to worship as we should. The Father wants this kind of worship from us. But you Samaritans know so little about Him, worshiping blindly, while we Jews know all about Him, for salvation comes to the world through the Jews."

The woman said, "Well, at least I know that the Messiah will come—the one they call Christ—and when He does, He will explain everything to us."

Then Jesus told her, "I am the Messiah!" (John 4:20-26, Living New Testament)

Our Lord did not allow any secondary questions to sidetrack Him from the main issue. The woman asked where she should worship, on Mount Gerazim or in Jerusalem, but Jesus steered the discussion back to Himself by shifting the emphasis from where to how one worships. Though hers was probably a legitimate question (her attitude was similar to the current honest question that many people have, "Which church should I join?"), our Lord refused to go off on a tangent; He left no doubt about the main issue: Himself.

Bring people to a direct confrontation with Christ

And finally, in declaring that He was the Messiah, our Lord reached the crucial point of the Gospel. Likewise, whether we spend one of many sessions building a bridge of friendship between us, we must eventually cross this bridge and bring the non-Christian into a direct confrontation with the Lord Jesus so that he realizes his personal responsibility to decide *for or against*—Him.

The people to whom we witness will fall into one of two categories initially. The first group includes those who lack the necessary information about Jesus Christ. Even if they wanted to, they wouldn't know how to become Christians. With such a person we should be alert, first, to discover the misunderstandings and gaps in their knowledge, and second, to seize each opportunity to explain more of the necessary facts.

Those in the second group are already informed about the Gospel, but they haven't acted on their information yet. Our repeated thumping of the same strings and continued cramming of the same information down their throats is more apt to alienate than to win them. When we know that an individual is fully informed about the Gospel, we should keep quiet, pray earnestly and daily for him by name, and love him into the kingdom of God.

These, then, are our seven principles—see and know non-Christians personally; establish a mutual interest in conversation; arouse a person's interest by life and word; gear explanations to his receptiveness and readiness for more; accept and even compliment rather than condemn; stay on the track; and persevere to the destination. Once we begin to grasp these principles and move out in faith, life becomes a daily fascination. We watch with anticipation to see the next opportunities God will give us to bear witness as ambassadors of Jesus Christ and to discover how He is working in the lives of others, through us.

Footnotes for the Living New Testament
paraphrase of John's Gospel

Footnotes for John 1:1—5:4

[a]Literally, "In the beginning."
[b]Literally, "the Word," meaning Christ, the wisdom and power of God and the first cause of all things; God's personal expression of Himself to men.
[c]Literally, "in the beginning."
[d]Literally, "to believe on His name."
[e]Literally, "not of blood."
[f]Literally, "the Word," meaning Christ, the wisdom and power of God and the first cause of all things; God's personal expression of Himself to men.
[g]Literally, "grace."
[h]See Matthew 17:2.
[i]Or, "His unique Son."
[j]Literally, "the Jews."
[k]See Deuteronomy 18:15.
[l]Or, "in."
[m]Literally, "the Son of Man." This was a name of great exaltation and glory.
[n]Literally, "Woman, what have I to do with you?"
[o]Literally, "His disciples believed on Him."
[p]Literally, "the Jews."
[q]Or, "Physical birth is not enough. You must also be born spiritually...." This alternate paraphrase interprets "born of water" as meaning the normal process observed during every human birth.
[r]Literally, "the Son of Man."
[s]Or, "the unique Son of God."
[t]Literally, "about purification."
[u]Implied.
[v]Implied.
[w]Implied.
[x]Apparently to avoid the crowds.
[y]See John 2:23.
[z]Many of the ancient manuscripts omit the material within the parentheses.

Footnotes for John 5:5—10:25

[a]Implied. Literally, "sin no more."
[b]Implied. Literally, "My Father works even until now, and I work."
[c]Implied. However, most commentators believe the reference is to the witness of His Father. See verse 37.
[d]Literally, "Now the Passover, the feast of the Jews, was at hand."
[e]Literally, 200 denarii, a denarius being a full day's wage.
[f]Literally, "and straightway the boat was at the land..."
[g]Implied.
[h]Literally, "the Son of Man."
[i]Implied.
[j]Implied.

[k]Implied. Literally, "Son of Man."
[l]Literally, "It is the Spirit who quickens."
[m]See John 1:13. Literally, "the flesh profits nothing."
[n]Literally, "I go not up (yet) unto this feast." The word "yet" is included in the text of many ancient manuscripts.
[o]Implied.
[p]Literally, "This multitude is accursed."
[q]Most ancient manuscripts omit John 7:53-8:11.
[r]Literally, "the Father."
[s]Literally, "when you have lifted up the Son of Man."
[t]Implied.
[u]Implied. Literally, "There is one that seeketh and judgeth."
[v]i.e., on Saturday, the weekly Jewish holy day when all work was forbidden.
[w]Literally, "you were altogether born in sin."
[x]Literally, "the Son of Man."
[y]December 25 was the usual date for this celebration of the cleansing of the Temple.
[z]Chapter 5:19; 8:36,56,58, etc., etc.

Footnotes for John 10:26—16:30

[a]Literally, "many believed on Him there."
[b]See John 12:3.
[c]Literally, "Whoever lives and believes on Me shall never die."
[d]Philip's name was Greek, though he was a Jew.
[e]Literally, "If any man."
[f]Implied. See II Corinthians 4:4, and Ephesians 2:2 and 6:12.
[g]Implied.
[h]Literally, "sons of light."
[i]Literally, "To whom has the arm of the Lord been revealed?" Isaiah 53:1.
[j]Literally, "He" Isaiah 6:10. The Greek here is a very free rendering, or paraphrase, of the original Hebrew.
[k]As the lowliest of slaves would dress.
[l]Implied. Literally, "whomsoever I send."
[m]Literally, "There was one at the table." All commentators believe him to be John, the writer of this book.
[n]Literally, "reclining on Jesus' bosom." The custom of the period was to recline around the table, leaning on the left elbow. John, next to Jesus, was at His side.
[o]Literally, "leaning back against Jesus' chest," to whisper his inquiry.
[p]Literally, "He it is for whom I shall dip the sop and give it him." The honored guest was thus singled out in the custom of that time.
[q]Or, "Advocate," or, "Lawyer."
[r]Literally, "in My name."
[s]Implied.
[t]Implied.
[u]Implied.
[v]Literally, "none of you is asking Me whither I am going." The question had been asked before (John 13:36, 14:5), but apparently not in this deeper sense.
[w]Literally, "He will convict the world of sin and righteousness and judgment."
[x]Implied.

231

^yLiterally, "you shall ask in My name." The above paraphrase is the modern equivalent of this idea, otherwise obscure.

^zLiterally, "and need not that anyone should ask you," i.e., discuss what is true.

Footnotes for John 16:31—21:7

^aLiterally, "kept in Your name those whom You have given Me."

^bLiterally, "the Praetorium."

^cBy Jewish law, entering the house of a Gentile was a serious offense.

^dLiterally, "It is not lawful for us to put any man to death."

^eThis prophecy is recorded in Matthew 20:19, which indicates His death by crucifixion, a practice under Roman law.

^fA paraphrase of this verse—that goes beyond the limits of this book's paraphrasing—would be, "Do you mean their King, or their Messiah?" If Pilate was asking as the Roman governor, he would be inquiring whether Jesus was setting up a rebel government. But the Jews were using the word "King" to mean their religious ruler, the Messiah. Literally this verse reads, "Are you saying this of yourself, or did someone else say it about me?"

^gImplied.

^hLiterally, "he."

ⁱLiterally, "the judgment seat in a place that is called The Pavement, but in Hebrew, Gabbatha."

^jPsalm 22:18.

^kLiterally, "standing by the disciple whom He loved."

^lLiterally, "to the disciple."

^mLiterally, "had received."

ⁿLiterally, "And he who has seen has borne witness, and his witness is true; and he knows what he says is true, that you also may believe."

^oSee chapter 3.

^pLiterally, "a garden."

^qLiterally, "on the first day of the week."

^rLiterally, "the other disciple whom Jesus loved."

^sLiterally, "Peter and the other disciple."

^tLiterally, "the other disciple also, who came first."

^uImplied.

^vLiterally, "the disciples."

^wImplied.

^xLiterally, "the sons of Zebedee."

^yLiterally, "children."

^zLiterally, "that disciple therefore whom Jesus loved."

Footnotes for John 21:7—21:25

^aImplied.

^bLiterally, "more than these." See Mark 14:29.

^cLiterally, "all things."

^dImplied. Literally, "and this man, what?"

^eLiterally, "tarry."